PERTAINING TO
Life and Godliness

ANTHONY SLUZAS

Pertaining to
Life and Godliness

Anthony Sluzas

All rights reserved. No part of this book may be reproduced or transmitted in any form or by any means, electronic or mechanical, or information storage and retrieval system without written permission from the author.

Unless otherwise indicated, all Scripture quotations are taken from **New King James Version of the Holy Bible**, Copyright © 1982 by Thomas Nelson. Used by permission. All rights reserved.

Copyright © 2020 by Anthony Sluzas.

ISBN: 979-8650419785

Printed in the United States of America.

Cover, interior design, and editing by:
The Righteous Pen Publications Group
The righteousness of God shall guide my pen
www.righteouspenpublications.com

*Grace and peace be multiplied to you in the knowledge of God
and of Jesus our Lord, as His divine power has given to us all things
that pertain to life and godliness, through the knowledge
of Him Who called us by glory and virtue, by which have been given
to us exceedingly great and precious promises, that through these
you may be partakers of the divine nature, having escaped
the corruption that is in the world through lust.*
(2 Peter 1:2-4)

Table of Contents

	Acknowledgments	i
1	Can I Believe and Base My Life Upon What the Bible Says?	1
2	Just Who is Satan?	9
3	Are the Ten Commandments for Today or Passé?	17
4	Rescued From the Inferno	27
5	Isn't the Concept of Obedience Really Just Legalism?	37
6	Counterfeits, False Religions, and Spirituality	45
7	Marriage By-the-Book	53
8	Do You Really Trust God?	65
9	Love That Transforms	73
10	I Have Decided to Follow Jesus… No Turning Back	83
	About the Author	91

Acknowledgements

I dedicate this book through a word of encouragement to my children, Jacob and Katie and her husband, Cory. I also dedicate this book to my precious grandsons, Carter and Nolan. Always keep your eyes upon Jesus. He will direct your paths, and "He Who began a good work in you will be faithful to complete it."

I also want to thank the Lord for reaching down, saving, healing, and delivering me from unforgiveness, bitterness and terrible substance abuse back in 1988.

Therefore, if anyone is in Christ, he is a new creation; old things have passed away; behold, all things have become new.
(2 Corinthians 5:17)

1
CAN I BELIEVE AND BASE MY LIFE UPON WHAT THE BIBLE SAYS?

DURING these crazy days of upheaval in the world, promises of stability and security are rarely, if ever, realized. Corrupt lying, cheating, and stealing politicians are running amok. The people you trust and depend on the most often hurt you the deepest. Where do you go, to whom do you turn, and what do you do? In our present day and age, when things are rapidly changing (not necessarily for the better), is there anything left that we can truly trust?

Yes, of course! You can fully trust the Bible; the infallible, inerrant Word of the living God. Let's investigate the evidence.

<u>What exactly does the Word of God claim about itself?</u>

The Bible unequivocally states:

All Scripture is inspired by God and is profitable for teaching, for reproof, for correction, and for instruction in righteousness. (2 Timothy 3:16)

For no prophecy at any time was produced by the will of man, but holy men moved by the Holy Spirit spoke from God. (1

Peter 1:21)

The Word of God is divinely inspired by Almighty God, and written by men, who were directed by the Holy Spirit. Its messages and great and precious promises cannot be broken or proved untrue. Every single book of the Bible from Genesis to Revelation points to the Lord Jesus Christ, and His death on the cross, burial, and resurrection.

Jesus demonstrated His belief in divine scripture and its power when He said:

It is written, 'Man shall not live by bread alone, but by every word that proceeds out of the mouth of God'... It is also written, 'You shall not tempt the Lord your God'... 'You shall worship the Lord your God, and Him only shall you serve.' (Matthew 4:4,7,10)

Sanctify them by Your truth. Your word is truth. (John 17:17)

Jesus boldly quoted from Scripture (the sword of the Spirit) when He was tempted by Satan in the wilderness. He also said that the Bible is truth—absolute truth (John 17:17). The Lord Jesus quoted the Word of God as the final authority for everything He was teaching.

What about prophecy?

It's understandable that many people in our day are very curious about Bible prophecy. Questions are frequently asked as to how Bible prophecies confirm its divine inspiration. God speaks ever so clearly on the subject:

I am the Lord... new things I declare, and before they spring forth, I tell you of them. (Isaiah 42:8-9).

I am God... declaring the end from the beginning and from ancient times, the things that are not yet done. (Isaiah 46:9-10)

There are hundreds of scriptural predictions regarding future events that have come to pass in dramatic fashion, and have confirmed the divine inspiration of the Bible. Here are just a few examples of prophecy fulfilled:

- There would be four major world empires that would arise: Babylon, Medo-Persia, Greece, and Rome (Daniel, chapters 2,7,8).
- The great Cyrus would be the mighty warrior who conquers Babylon (Isaiah 45:1-3).
- Following Babylon's total destruction, it would never be inhabited by people again (Isaiah 13: 19,20; Jeremiah 51:37).
- Never again in history would Egypt hold a dominant position among the nations of the world (Ezekiel 29:14-15; 30:12-13).
- Rampant immorality and false religions will spread across the planet in the last days (2 Timothy 3:1-5).
- Earth shaking calamities and disasters will come, causing increasing anxiety among nations and individuals. Hearts will literally fail people for fear (Luke 21:25-26).

What about science?

Many more folks in our day are skeptical, even hostile, and wonder aloud if the Bible's claims about the natural world are actually confirmed by science. Are they? Absolutely. Psalm 119:160 tells us that *The entirety of Your Word is truth.* Yes, friends, the Holy Spirit, Who guided each and every Bible writer, always speaks the truth. Here are just several out of many statements from God's Word that are confirmed by science:

It is He who sits upon the circle of the earth. (Isaiah 40:22)

The Word of God said that the earth was round many centuries before it was confirmed by science!

He hangs the earth upon nothing. (Job 26:7)

This is a scientific fact mentioned in the book of Job, the oldest in the Bible.

To make the weight of the wind. (Job 28:25)

Centuries before it was verified by science, the Bible stated that air has weight.

What about well-being?

Everyone is concerned about their health, nutrition, and exercise these days. Are the statements in the Word of God regarding health still relevant in the 21st century? The Bible says:

Beloved, I pray that all may go well with you and that you may be in good health, even as your soul is prospers. (3 John 1:2)

Yes, it's true that our Heavenly Father wants His children to be genuinely happy and healthy. Let's look at a few more scriptural examples of the Bible's health principles confirming its divine inspiration:

- Completely cover over bodily wastes with dirt. (Deuteronomy 23:12-13) Moses commanded that bodily wastes be buried outside the encampment of Israel. This concept was thousands of years ahead of its time. When human waste isn't properly disposed, disease can rapidly spread through the water supply. This Bible rule has literally saved millions of lives throughout history.

- Leave the booze and drugs alone. (Proverbs 23:29-32) Think about it. If everyone obeyed this scriptural admonition, millions of substance abusers would become clean, sober, and helpful citizens. Millions of dysfunctional and broken families would be reconciled and reunited. Countless lives would be saved from drunk driving, while government and business leaders would make clear-minded and wise decisions.

- Flee sexual immorality. (1 Corinthians 10:8) The term "sexual immorality" in the Bible refers to any inappropriate sexual conduct outside marriage between man and wife (see Leviticus 18 for a complete list). By following this Bible counsel, folks would have little reason to be afraid of unwanted pregnancies or sexually transmitted diseases which can sometimes turn deadly... as well as the sin of abortion.

What about history?

Is the Bible accurate in regard to historical statements throughout its pages? God says, *I, the Lord, speak righteousness; I declare things that are right.* (Isaiah 45:19) Take note the following points of fact:

- Skeptics have said that the Bible came from the imaginations and fertile minds of mere men and it's unreliable because it mentions the Hittite nation (Deuteronomy 7:1) and cities like Sodom (Genesis 19:1), and Nineveh (Jonah 1:1-2), all of which they've denied ever existed. However, over the years, we've seen how modern archaeology has confirmed that all three did exist.

- Skeptics have claimed that the Bible record of Moses wasn't reliable because it speaks of writing (Exodus 24:4) and vehicles with wheels (Exodus 14:25) which they claim didn't exist at that time. However, today, we know that they absolutely did exist.

- At one point in history, the thirty-nine kings of ancient Israel and Judah were known only from the Bible. Thus, once again, critics cast outright doubt their existence. But when archaeologists discovered independent ancient records that mention many of these kings, the Biblical record was proven accurate once again. God's Word doesn't merely contain truth; it is truth.

What else can we see from the Bible?

Many more undeniable truths about the Word of God prove its divine inspiration. The scripture declares:

All Scripture is inspired by God. (2 Timothy 3:16)

Please consider, if you will, that all 66 books of the Bible were written:

- In three languages.
- On three continents.
- By some forty very different people (shepherds, kings, lawyers, a doctor, a general, scientists, priests, and a fisherman).
- Over a fifteen-hundred-year period.
- By men whose backgrounds and educations were radically different.
- On the most controversial subjects.

Miraculously, these sixty-six books of the Bible maintain perfect harmony with one another. Yes, again, it is truly miraculous. The Word of God, which was penned by forty writers over a fifteen-hundred-year period, reads as if it was written by one mind—because, in reality, it was!

For no prophecy at any time was produced by the will of man, but holy men moved by the Holy Spirit spoke from God. (2 Peter 1:21)

Finally, the evidence of the divine inspiration of God's Word is found in the lives of millions of people, up to this very day. The Bible says:

Therefore, if any man is in Christ, he is a new creature. Old things have passed away. Look, all things have become new. (2 Corinthians 5:17)

The radically changed lives of those who have given their hearts and lives to Jesus Christ and who obey God's Word are some of the most convincing proofs of the divine inspiration and infallibility of the Bible. The substance abuser, like I was, gets clean and sober; the immoral person is forgiven, and becomes pure; the one in chains of bondage is delivered; the fearful person becomes courageous; and the cruel person becomes kind and loving.

We must feed upon God's Word daily. We've no problem with feeding our bodies. Get God's Word deep inside your spirit being! It is your best chance for true, lasting happiness, peace, and fulfillment. The Bible tells us:

Your Word is a lamp to my feet and a light to my path. (Psalm 119:105)

I have spoken these things to you, that My joy may remain in you, and that your joy may be full. (John 15:11)

Let your light so shine before men that they may see your good works and glorify your Father Who is in heaven. (Matthew 5:16)

I will come again and receive you to Myself, that where I am, you may be also. (John 14:3)

There is so much more God desires to show all of us as we sojourn through this life on earth together. Let's make the most of it as we walk hand-in-hand with Jesus. Yes, dear one, there truly is so much more to learn "pertaining to life and godliness." Read on, my friend. Read on.

Anthony Sluzas

2
JUST WHO IS SATAN?

WHAT'S up with this malevolent creature the Bible calls "Satan?" Is he, as some scoffers claim, just a mythical figure someone with a fertile mind dreamed up long ago? The Word of God teaches us that the devil is indeed very real and that he is determined to deceive us and destroy you lives. Make no mistake about it, the evil one is a brilliant mastermind who is entrapping human beings, their families, churches, and even entire nations, whose endgame is to wreak havoc, sorrow, and pain in this world.

Lucifer

Sin originated with Lucifer, originally a beautifully exotic and gifted angel of God. The Bible tells us:

The devil has been sinning from the beginning. (1 John 3:8)

That ancient serpent called the Devil and Satan. (Revelation 12:9)

Satan's name was Lucifer, and he used to live in heaven. Lucifer is also symbolized by the "king of Babylon" in Isaiah 15 and as the "prince of Tyre" in Ezekiel 28.

How are you fallen from heaven, O Lucifer, son of the morning! How you are cut down to the ground, you who weaken the nations! (Isaiah 14:12)

Then again, in Ezekiel 28:14:

You were the anointed cherub that covers, and I set you there; you were upon the holy mountain of God; you walked up and down in the midst of the stones of fire.

We then see this in the New Testament:

He (Jesus) said to them, "I saw Satan as lightning fall from heaven." (Luke 10:18)

You were on the holy mountain of God. (Ezekiel 28:14)

Who was this Lucifer, and how is he described?

You were created. (Ezekiel 28:15)

You were the seal of perfection, full of wisdom and perfect in beauty... Every precious stone was your covering... The workmanship of your timbrels and pipes was prepared for you on the day you were created... You were perfect in your ways from the day you were created, until iniquity was found in you. (Ezekiel 28:12,13,15)

You were the anointed cherub who covers; I established you. You were on the holy mountain of God; you walked back and forth in the midst of fiery stones. (Ezekiel 28:14)

Lucifer was created by Almighty God, as were all of the angels (Ephesians 3:9). This magnificent creature, Lucifer, was a "covering" angel or cherub. One covering angel stands on the left of the throne of God, and the other on the right (Psalm 99:1). Lucifer was a highly exalted angel and he was a leader. His beauty was breathtaking, even flawless, and his wisdom was vast. His brightness was awe-inspiring. Ezekiel 28:13 indicates he was specially created to be an outstanding musician. Some theologians believe the Word of God intimates that he led the angelic choir... a worship leader.

What changed inside Lucifer, and what sin did he commit?

Your heart was lifted up because of your beauty; you corrupted your wisdom for the sake of your splendor. (Ezekiel 28:17)

For you have said in your heart: 'I will ascend into heaven, I will exalt my throne above the stars of God... I will be like the Most High.' (Isaiah 14:13,14)

Pride, discontent, and jealousy metastasized in Lucifer's heart as he actually desired to unseat the God of the universe and demand that everyone worship him instead.

Many people have asked me over the years, why is worship such a big deal? The answer is that worship is the key factor in the ages-old conflict between God and the wicked one. Human beings were created by God to be happy, strengthened, and fulfilled when we worship Him with all of our heart. Not even the angels of heaven, nor dead saints, nor our deceased relatives are to be prayed to or worshiped. This is strictly forbidden (Revelation 22:8-9). Satan selfishly sought this worship that's due only to God, and God alone. Many centuries later, when he tempted Jesus in the wilderness, worship was still Satan's desire and a key test (Matthew 4:8-11). As we are now in the last of the last days, as God calls upon all people to worship Him (Revelation 14:6-7), this so infuriates the devil that he will try to force people to worship himself or else be martyred (Revelation 13:15).

The truth is, that literally every person on the planet worships someone or something: money, career, prestige, power, pleasure, food, possessions, etc. However, Almighty God says:

You shall have no other gods before Me. (Exodus 20:3)

Just like the fallen Lucifer, you and I have a choice about whom we worship. If we choose to worship anyone or anything other than God, He will most assuredly honor our choice, but we will be counted among the number of those who have turned against Him (Matthew 12:30). Again, if anyone or anything other than God receives first place in our lives, we will end up following in Satan's footsteps toward perdition. Does God hold the position of being first place in your life, or are you serving the wicked one (whether you realize it or not)? There is no middle ground. Granted, it's a sobering question, but one that you must answer. This may very well be your hour of decision.

Literal war broke out in heaven as a consequence of Lucifer's rebellion.

Michael and his angels fought with the dragon; and the dragon and his angels fought, but they did not prevail, nor was a place found for them in heaven any longer. So, the great dragon was cast out, that serpent of old, called the Devil and Satan, who deceives the whole world; he was cast to the earth, and his angels were cast out with him. (Revelation 12:7-9)

The Bible tells us that the fallen one, Lucifer, deceived one-third of the angels (Revelation 12:3-4) and caused a rebellion in heaven. Our God had to cast out Lucifer and the other fallen angels because Lucifer's aim was to usurp God's throne (John 8:44). After his expulsion from heaven, Lucifer was called Satan, which means "adversary," and the devil, meaning "slanderer." The angels who cast in their lot with Satan were called demons.

What is Satan doing now?

Many people wonder where Satan specifically is and what he's up to in our day.

And the Lord said to Satan, 'From where do you come?' Satan answered the Lord and said, 'From going to and fro on the earth, and from walking back and forth on it.' (Job 2:2)

Woe to the inhabitants of the earth and the sea! For the devil has come down to you, having great wrath, because he knows that he has a short time. (Revelation 12:12)

Be sober, be vigilant; because your adversary the devil walks about like a roaring lion, seeking whom he may devour. (1 Peter 5:8).

Contrary to widespread belief due to ignorance of God's Word and improper teaching, Satan's headquarters is planet earth, not hell. We find in Genesis that God gave Adam and Eve dominion over the earth (Genesis 1:26). When they sinned, committing high treason against God by bowing the knee to the evil one, they lost this dominion to Satan (Romans 6:16). It was at that moment when the adversary became the ruler, or 'god' of this world (John 12:31). Satan despises all of humanity, we who were created in the image and likeness of God. Since it is impossible to harm God directly, he directs his anger against the human race on the earth. He's a hateful murderer whose aim is to destroy you, and thus wanting to hurt God.

When God created Adam and Eve, He gave them dominion over everything on this planet. However, there was one thing the Lord commanded them not to do.

But of the tree of the knowledge of good and evil you shall not eat, for in the day that you eat of it you shall surely die. (Genesis 2:17).

Remember, God created Adam and Eve with His own hands and placed them in a beautifully exotic garden where they could enjoy eating the fruit from every kind of tree...except just one (Genesis 2:7-9). This was the Lord God graciously giving them a fair choice. If they would but trust God, obey and not eat of the forbidden tree, they would live forever in paradise. However, by choosing to listen to Satan, they chose to run away from the Source of all life—God—and naturally experienced death.

The Bible tells us that the woman was deceived, but the man was not. The man just outright disobeyed.

Now the serpent was more cunning than any beast of the field which the Lord God had made. And he said to the woman, "Has God indeed said, 'You shall not eat of every tree of the garden'?" Now the serpent was more cunning than any beast of the field which the Lord God had made. And he said to the woman, "Has God indeed said, 'You shall not eat of every tree of the garden'?" (Genesis 3:1,4,5)

We see that Satan adopted the form of a serpent, one of the

wisest, most exotic and beautiful creatures God had made. Today, some scholars believe that the serpent originally had wings and flew (Isaiah 14:29; 30:6). Keep in mind that the serpent did not crawl until God cursed it (Genesis 3:14). Satan's lies were:

- You won't die, and
- Eating the fruit will make you wise.

Satan, the father of lies (John 8:44), mixed truth with the lies he told Eve. Lies which include some truth are the most effective deceptions (and this unfortunately, is prevalent in the world today). It actually was true that they would "know evil" after sinning. Because of His great love, God had withheld the knowledge of evil from them, which includes heartache, grief, suffering, pain, and death. Satan made the knowledge of evil appear attractive and very desirable, telling lies to misrepresent God's character. The adversary knows that people will be more likely to turn away from a loving God if they misunderstand or are confused about His character.

The question is still asked to this very day: Why was eating a piece of fruit such a bad and tragic thing, causing the first couple to be removed from the garden? God's Word clearly answers this question:

Therefore, to him who knows to do good and does not do it, to him it is sin. (James 4:17)

Whoever commits sin also commits lawlessness, and sin is lawlessness. (1 John 3:4)

Then the Lord God said, "Behold, the man has become like one of Us, to know good and evil. And now, lest he put out his hand and take also of the tree of life, and eat, and live forever"... So, He drove out the man; and He placed cherubim at the east of the garden of Eden, and a flaming sword which turned every way, to guard the way to the tree of life. (Genesis 3:22,24)

Eating the forbidden fruit was a sin because it was an outright rejection of one of God's few requirements. It was open rebellion against God's law and authority. By rejecting God's command, Adam and Eve chose to follow Satan, therefore causing separation between themselves and God (Isaiah 59:2). Satan very likely hoped the couple would continue eating from the tree of life after their sin, thus becoming immortal sinners, but God removed them from the garden to prevent this from happening.

From the creation until now, Satan's temptations and evil strategies continue to be effective in the world. The wicked one convinced one-third of the angels (Revelation 12:3-9); Adam and Eve (Genesis 3), and all but eight people in Noah's day (1 Peter 3:20). Almost the entire world follows him instead of Jesus Christ (Revelation 13:3). Many will be forever separated from God and in hell because of the devil's lies (Matthew 7:14; 22:14).

The success rate of the adversary is alarmingly high, but this is only temporary. Remember, he deceived one-third of heaven's angels. In the days of Noah, all but eight people on the earth were deceived. We are told that before Jesus' second coming, Satan will appear to have full control of the planet. His deceptive power will be so great that our only safety will be in resisting him (Matthew 24:23-26). If you refuse to listen to him, Jesus will protect you from Satan's deceptions (John 10:29).

What lies ahead?

Satan's eternal punishment and that of those who reject Jesus Christ as Savoir and Lord is coming, and it is sure.

And it will be so at the end of this age. The Son of Man will send out His angels, and they will gather out of His kingdom all things that offend, and those who practice lawlessness, and will cast them into the furnace of fire. (Matthew 13:40-42)

The devil, who deceived them, was cast into the lake of fire and brimstone. (Revelation 20:10)

Depart from Me, you cursed, into the everlasting fire prepared for the devil and his angels. (Matthew 25:41)

I brought fire from your midst; it devoured you, and I turned you to ashes upon the earth in the sight of all who saw you.

All who knew you among the peoples are astonished at you; you have become a horror, and shall be no more forever. (Ezekiel 28:18-19).

Satan will be cast into the lake of fire at the end of the age, at the culmination of all things. God will deal with the evil one for his sin, for tempting others to sin, and for hurting and destroying the people whom God loves.
    The good news is that sin will be eradicated completely, and it will never rise up again.

At the name of Jesus every knee should bow, of those in heaven, and of those on earth, and of those under the earth, and that every tongue should confess that Jesus Christ is Lord, to the glory of God the Father. (Philippians 2:10-11).

Affliction will not rise up a second time. (Nahum 1:9)

Two monumental events will finally settle the problem of sin. The first monumental event will occur when all beings in heaven and earth, including Satan and his demonic hordes, will bow the knee before God and openly confess that He is truth, and He is just. He is fair and righteous. There will be no questions unanswered. All sinners who have rejected the Lord Jesus Christ as Savior and Lord will be lost. Every mouth will be silenced. They will know that they deserve eternal death. The second monumental event which will take place is the purging of sin from the universe by the permanent incarceration and destruction of all who have chosen their sin over Christ the Savior.
    Won't you open your heart to Jesus Christ today?

For this purpose, the Son of God was manifested, that He might destroy the works of the devil. (1 John 3:8)

Inasmuch then as the children have partaken of flesh and blood, He Himself likewise shared in the same, that through death He might destroy him who had the power of death, that is, the devil. (Hebrews 2:14)

Look up, loved one, your redemption draws near!

3

ARE THE TEN COMMANDMENTS FOR TODAY OR PASSÉ?

AS our modern-day media constantly bombards us with news of crime, plague, pestilence, violence, and natural disasters, doesn't it make sense that to secure and maintain peace and safety, that we should obey the laws of the land? Long, long ago, our Heavenly Father wrote His own law in stone—literally! The Bible clearly teaches that we are still supposed to keep it today. When we violate any part of God's commands, it will always bring about negative consequences. What's most important is that keeping God's laws secures our peace and safety. There's really so much at stake in choosing to be obedient or disobedient. Let's take just a few minutes to consider the place of God's Ten Commandments in our lives in the 21st century.

The Bible teaches that the God of heaven wrote the Ten Commandments on tablets of stone with His own finger.

He gave Moses two tablets of the Testimony, tablets of stone, written with the finger of God...Now the tablets were the work of God, and the writing was the writing of God engraved on the tablets. (Exodus 31:18; 32:16)

What is God's definition of sin?

The Bible says:

Sin is lawlessness. (1 John 3:4)

Sin is breaking any one or more of God's Ten Commandments. The law of God is perfect (Psalm 19:7), and its principles cover every conceivable sin. These commandments cover all and the entire duty of man (Ecclesiastes 12:13). There is nothing left out. Sin also occurs when we knowingly fail to do the good that God would have us to do.

Why did the Lord give humanity the Ten Commandments in the first place?

Where there is no revelation, the people cast off restraint but happy is he who keeps the law. (Proverbs 29:18)

My son, do not forget my law, but let your heart keep my commands; for length of days and long life and peace they will add to you. (Proverbs 3:1-2)

God's law is a road map that points out the right path to follow to find true fulfillment and happiness.

By the law is knowledge of sin. (Romans 3:20)

I would not have known sin except through the law. For I would not have known covetousness unless the law had said, "You shall not covet." (Romans 7:7)

God created us to experience happiness, peace, long life, contentment, accomplishment, fulfillment and all the other great blessings for which our hearts long—if we will honor and obey His laws. Again, we could describe the law of God as a diagnostic tool that points out wrongdoing in our lives much like a mirror points out dirt or blemishes on our faces (James 1:23-25). The only possible way for us to know we are sinning is to carefully examine our lives by the mirror of God's Word. Peace for a mixed-up, sin-sick world can be found in only in a personal relationship with Jesus Christ, and the Word of God. It tells us just exactly where to draw the line.

The Lord commanded us to observe all these statutes, to fear the Lord our God, for our good always. (Deuteronomy 6:24)

Hold me up, and I shall be safe, and I shall observe Your statutes continually. You reject all those who stray from Your statutes, for their deceit is falsehood. (Psalm 119:117-118)

The Commandments protect us from danger and tragedy. The law of God is like a strong and secure cage at a zoo that protects us from fierce, dangerous animals. The Word of God protects us from idolatry, murder, lies, theft, and a myriad of other evils that destroy life, peace, and happiness. All good laws are designed to protect, and God's law is no exception.

By this we know that we know Him, if we keep His commandments. (1 John 2:3)

The Bible tells us the eternal principles within God's law are written deep within every person's heart by the God who created us. Though the ink on the page may be dim and smudged with the passing of time, it is still there. We were created to live obediently and in harmony with them. When we ignore them, the result is always unrest, tension, and tragedy—just as ignoring the laws of safe driving can lead to serious injury or ultimately death.

God's precepts are extremely important to every human being:

So, speak and so do as those who will be judged by the law of liberty. (James 2:12)

<u>An everlasting standard</u>

The Ten Commandments are the standard by which God examines the hearts of people, and they are still in effect in New Testament days. They've never passed away. Jesus taught us to obey them.

It is easier for heaven and earth to pass away than for one tittle of the law to fail. (Luke 16:17)

My covenant I will not break, nor alter the word that has gone out of My lips. (Psalm 89:34)

All His precepts are sure. They stand fast forever and ever. (Psalm 111:7-8)

Let's be crystal clear: The Bible says the law of God cannot be changed. This means that the Ten Commandments are revealed principles of God's holy character and are the very foundation of His Kingdom. These principles will be true and remain as long as God exists—which will be forever! It is no more possible to change God's law than to pull God out of heaven and change Him. The Lord Jesus Christ showed us what the law—that is, the pattern for righteous and holy living looks like when it's expressed in human form. The perfect character of God cannot change; therefore, neither can His law.

There are those in our day who declare we are no longer obligated to live by the Ten Commandments. How mistaken these people are. Did Jesus abolish the Commandments while He was here on earth? Absolutely not. Our Lord said:

Do not think that I came to destroy the Law... I did not come to destroy, but to fulfill... till heaven and earth pass away, one jot or one tittle will by no means pass from the law till all is fulfilled. (Matthew 5:17-18)

Jesus specifically and on purpose asserted that He did not come to destroy the law, but to fulfill it. Instead of doing away with the law, Jesus magnified and reaffirmed it (Isaiah 42:21) as the perfect guide for holy living. As an example of this, we see that Jesus pointed out that:

- *You shall not murder* condemns anger "without a cause" (Matthew 5:21-22) and hatred (1 John 3:15).

- Lust is a form of adultery (Matthew 5:27-28).

- He also said, *If you love Me, keep My commandments*

(John 14:15).

The Word of God repeatedly warns us about the dangers of sin.

The wages of sin are death. (Romans 6:23)

Behold, the day of the Lord comes, cruel, with both wrath and fierce anger, to lay the land desolate; and He will destroy its sinners. (Isaiah 13:9)

Whoever shall keep the whole law, and yet stumble in one point, he is guilty of all. (James 2:10)

God's law within the Ten Commandments guides us into holy living. Should we choose to ignore even one of the commandments, we neglect an essential part of the divine blueprint, and thus become a law breaker. If just one single, solitary link of a chain is broken, its entire purpose is undone. The Bible states that when we knowingly break a command of God, we are sinning (James 4:17) because we have refused His will for us. Only those who do the will of God can enter the kingdom of heaven. Of course, God will forgive anyone who genuinely turns from their sins and accepts the person and power of the Lord Jesus Christ to change him or her.

Can we be saved by the law?

Can anyone be saved and make it to heaven by keeping the law? In a word—No.

Therefore, by the deeds of the law no flesh will be justified in His sight, for by the law is the knowledge of sin. (Romans 3:20)

For by grace you have been saved through faith, and that not of yourselves; it is the gift of God, not of works, lest anyone should boast. (Ephesians 2:8-9).

No one can be saved by keeping the law, because it is impossible for any sinful human being to perfectly keep the law. Break God's law at just one point, and you've broken it all. You've become a law breaker. Salvation comes only by grace, as a free gift of Jesus Christ, and we receive this gift by faith, not by our works. The law serves as a mirror that graphically points out the filth and grime of sin in our lives. Just as a mirror can reveal dirt, blemishes, or scars on your face but cannot clean your face, so cleansing and forgiveness from that sin come only through Christ and what He did for you at the Cross. It's a free gift.

The full pattern, or whole duty of Christian living is found in the Word of God. Like a little child who made his own ruler and measured himself, then told his mama he was ten feet tall, our own standards of measure are never safe. We cannot know whether we are sinners unless we look carefully into the perfect standard—God's law. Many mistakenly think that by doing good works alone, it will "earn" them a spot in heaven even if they ignore God's Word and standard. (Matthew 7:21-23). Hence, they think they are righteous and saved when in fact, they are sinful and lost.

Now by this we know that we know Him, if we keep His commandments. (1 John 2:3)

What enables a newly saved believer to obey and live by the Word of God?

I will put My laws in their mind and write them on their hearts. (Hebrews 8:10)

I can do all things through Christ Who strengthens me. (Philippians 4:13)

God did by sending His own Son... that the righteous requirement of the law might be fulfilled in us. (Romans 8:3-4).

Due to His sacrifice on the cross, Jesus Christ not only pardons repentant sinners, He also restores them in the image of Almighty God when they are born again. He brings them into harmony with the law through the power of His indwelling Spirit. Thus, He now lives in us and is in control as we yield to His perfect will. God will not change His moral law, but He's made provision through Jesus' finished work at the Cross to change the sinner from the inside-out, so we can live righteously.

Many will ask if the Christian who puts their faith in Christ and is now living under grace freed from the law?

Sin is lawlessness. (1 John 3:4)

Sin shall not have dominion over you... Shall we sin because we are not under law but under grace? Certainly not! (Romans 6:14-15)

On the contrary, we establish the law. (Romans 3:31)

Let's put it this way: Grace is like a governor's pardon to a prison inmate. Said pardon forgives him, but it doesn't give him the freedom to break another law. The forgiven person living under grace will actually want to keep God's precepts in his or her great gratitude for salvation. The person who refuses to keep God's Commandments because he is claiming that he's now living under grace, is sorely mistaken.

The law and the New Covenant

Many misguided people, including lots of ministers, have said that the Ten Commandments are not applicable under the New Covenant. Wrong! Let's take a closer look...

You shall worship the Lord your God, and Him only you shall serve. (Matthew 4:10)

Little children, keep yourselves from idols. (1 John 5:21)

Since we are the offspring of God, we ought not to think that the Divine Nature is like gold or silver or stone, something shaped by art and man's devising. (Acts 17:29)

That the name of God and His doctrine may not be blasphemed. (1 Timothy 6:1)

He has spoken in a certain place of the seventh day in this way: "And God rested on the seventh day from all His works"... There remains therefore a rest for the people of God.

For he who has entered His rest has himself also ceased from his works as God did from His. (Hebrews 4:4,9-10)

Honor your father and your mother. (Matthew 19:19)

You shall not murder. (Romans 13:9)

You shall not commit adultery. (Matthew 19:18)

You shall not steal. (Romans 13:9)

You shall not bear false witness. (Romans 13:9)

You shall not covet. (Romans 7:7)

We need to make abundantly clear the fact that the law of Moses and the law of God are not the same. The law of Moses contained the temporary, ceremonial laws of the Old Covenant. It regulated the priesthood sacrifices, rituals, meat and drink offerings, etc., all of which foreshadowed and pointed toward the cross of Christ. The law was added "till the Seed should come," and that seed was Jesus Christ (Galatians 3:16,19). The ritual and ceremony of Moses' law pointed forward to Christ's ultimate sacrifice for all humanity. When He died, this law came to an end, but the Ten Commandments (God's law) "stand fast forever and ever" (Psalm 111:8). The fact that there are these two laws is made crystal clear in Daniel 9:10-11.
    Satan certainly hates the Ten Commandments, and especially those who make the decision to live by them.

And the dragon was enraged with the woman, and he went to make war with the rest of her offspring, who keep the commandments of God and have the testimony of Jesus Christ. (Revelation 12:17)

Here is the patience of the saints; here are those who keep the commandments of God and the faith of Jesus. (Revelation 14:12)

The adversary hates with a passion those who uphold God's law, because this law is a pattern of righteous living, and so it's not surprising that he bitterly opposes all who uphold God's Word. In his all-out war against God's holy standard, the devil goes so far as to use religious leaders to deny the Ten Commandments while at the same time, upholding the traditions of men. It's no wonder that Jesus said:

Why do you also transgress the commandment of God because of your tradition?...in vain they worship Me, teaching as doctrines the commandments of men. (Matthew 15:3,9)

David said:

It is time for You to act, O Lord, for they have regarded Your law as void. (Psalm 119:126)

Born again believers must awaken and restore God's law to its rightful place in their hearts and lives.

Anthony Sluzas

4
RESCUED FROM THE INFERNO

AT some point in your life, it's very likely that you have witnessed a terrible fire. Imagine if you will, the horror of being trapped in a house as flames and searing heat appear all around you as black choking smoke threatens to overcome you. Then imagine how incredibly grateful and relieved you would feel to be swiftly plucked up to safety. The truth of the matter is that every person on the planet is in serious danger. We all desperately and urgently need rescue, and not only by people in uniform, but by Almighty God. The Heavenly Father loves you so much that He sent His only begotten Son to die on the cross to save you. You've probably heard this before, but are you sure that you understand what it's really all about? What does it truly mean and can it literally change your life?

Far too many people openly ask the question, "Does God really care about me?" This is what He has said:

Since you were precious in My sight, you have been honored and I have loved you. (Isaiah 43:4)

Yes, I have loved you with an everlasting love. (Jeremiah 31:3).

God's never-ending love for you is far beyond puny human

understanding. He would love you even if you were the only lost soul on the planet. The Lord Jesus would have given His life for you on the cross, even if there had been no other sinner to save. Never forget that you are precious in His sight. He loves and cares about you deeply.

How much does God love us?

God has lovingly and powerfully demonstrated His love for you.

For God so loved the world that He gave His only begotten Son, that whoever believes in Him should not perish but have everlasting life. (John 3:16)

In this the love of God was manifested toward us, that God has sent His only begotten Son into the world, that we might live through Him. In this is love, not that we loved God, but that He loved us and sent His Son to be the propitiation for our sins. (1 John 4:9-10)

Because God loves you so deeply, He was willing to send His only Son to suffer and die on the cross for you rather than be separated from you for eternity. It would be impossible to grasp that kind of amazing, abundant love, but God did it for you, dear one! Jesus' sacrificial death on the cross for you was the greatest demonstration of love in the universe!

You even now might be asking, "How could God love someone like me?" Yes, a thousand times, YES!

God demonstrates His own love toward us, in that while we were still sinners, Christ died for us. (Romans 5:8)

You see, Jesus' great love for you is clearly seen in His willingness to forgive your sins and His desire to give you victory over every temptation in your life!

Love and salvation

Absolutely no one "deserves" salvation. Not one person has ever "earned" anything except the wages of sin, which is death (Romans 6:23). However, God's love is unconditional. He loves those people who have committed adultery, those who have stolen, those who are selfish and hypocritical, and those who are addicted. No matter what you have done or what you are doing, God loves you—and He wants to save you from sin and its deadly consequences.

What did the Lord Jesus Christ accomplish for you through His sacrificial death on the cross?

Behold what manner of love the Father has bestowed on us, that we should be called children of God! (1 John 3:1)

But as many as received Him, to them He gave the right to become children of God, to those who believe in His name. (John 1:12)

Jesus died to satisfy the wrath of God toward sin and the death penalty against you. He was God manifest in human flesh for the specific purpose that He would suffer the kind of death all sinners really deserve. Today, He offers to give you the credit for what He did. His sinless life is credited to you so that you can be counted righteous in the eyes of God. His sacrificial death was accepted by God as full payment for all your wrongs (past, present, future) and when you accept what He did as a gift, you are received into God's own family as His very own child.

How does one receive Jesus as personal Savior and pass from death to life? You must admit three things:

- I am a sinner (*All have sinned*, Romans 3:23).

- I am sentenced to die (*The wages of sin are death*, Romans 6:23).

- I cannot save myself (*Without Me you can do nothing*, John 15:5).

Next, believe these three truths:

- Jesus died for me (*That... He might taste death for everyone,* Hebrews 2:9).

- He forgives me (*If we confess our sins, He is faithful and just to forgive us our sins*, 1 John 1:9).

- He saves me (*He who believes in Me has everlasting life*, John 6:47)

Here are the hard facts:

- Because of my sins, I am under a death sentence.

- I cannot possibly pay this penalty and would be separated from God forever.

- I owe something I can't pay, but Jesus says, "I will pay the penalty. I will suffer and die in your place and give you credit for it. You will not have to die for your sins."

- I will accept His offer! The moment I acknowledge my debt and accept His death for my sins, I become His very own child!

Open your heart right now and receive!

[We] being justified freely by His grace through the redemption that is in Christ Jesus. (Romans 3:24).

Man is justified by faith apart from the deeds of the law. (Romans 3:28).

The gift of salvation

The only thing you can do is receive salvation as a gift... because it truly is just that! No matter how much one may try, rituals, ceremonies, rules, regulations, and works of obedience will not help anyone to be justified, because we have already sinned and deserve death. The good news is that all who ask in faith for salvation by receiving Jesus as Savior and Lord, will receive it! So, come to the cross of Christ! The worst reprobate is accepted just as completely as the one who sins the least. Your past does not count against you at the foot of the Cross. God loves everyone alike and forgiveness is simply for the asking.

For by grace you have been saved through faith, and that not of yourselves; it is the gift of God, not of works, lest anyone should boast. (Ephesians 2:8-9)

The moment you join the family of faith by accepting Jesus as Savior and Lord, what change does the Lord make in your life?

Therefore, if anyone is in Christ, he is a new creation; old things have passed away; behold, all things have become new. (2 Corinthians 5:17).

Upon receiving Jesus Christ into your heart, He begins the process of destroying your old sinful self and changing you into a new spiritual creation. The plug on the sin nature has been pulled, so to speak, in order to make it dormant. Joyfully, you begin to experience the glorious freedom from guilt and condemnation, and the old life of sin becomes repulsive to you. You'll see that one minute with God provides more happiness than a lifetime of being the devil's slave. What a wonderful exchange! Why do people wait for so long to accept it?

As a child of God, your life will be changed... and so will your attitude!

These things I have spoken to you, that My joy may remain in you, and that your joy may be full. (John 15:11)

If the Son makes you free, you shall be free indeed. (John 8:36)

I have come that they may have life, and that they may have it more abundantly. (John 10:10)

Many people feel the Christian life will not be a happy one because of self-denial. The exact opposite is true. When you accept the love of Jesus, His joy springs up within you. Even when hard times come, the Christian can enjoy God's strong, assuring, and powerful presence to overcome and "to help in time of need" (Hebrews 4:16).

Another common question that's asked is, "Can I really change and do I even have the power to do so?" The Bible answers:

I have been crucified with Christ; it is no longer I who live, but Christ lives in me. (Galatians 2:20)

I can do all things through Christ Who strengthens me. (Philippians 4:13).

It's not a burden to please someone you truly love.

If you love Me, keep My commandments. (John 14:15)

For this is the love of God, that we keep His commandments. And His commandments are not burdensome. (1 John 5:3)

Whoever keeps His word, truly the love of God is perfected in him. By this we know that we are in Him. (1 John 2:5)

The Bible ties obedience to a genuine love for God. Christians will not find it by wearying to keep the Commandments. With all your sins washed away by Jesus' atoning death on the Cross, your obedience is rooted in His victorious life within you. Because you love Him so deeply for changing your life, you will actually go beyond the requirements of the Ten Commandments by living the royal law of love.

The royal law of love

What is the royal law of love?

"Teacher, which is the great commandment in the law?" Jesus said to him, "'You shall love the Lord your God with all your heart, with all your soul, and with all your mind.' This is the first and great commandment. And the second is like it: 'You shall love your neighbor as yourself.' On these two commandments hang all the Law and the Prophets. (Matthew 22:36-40).

You will regularly search the Bible to know His will, trying to find more ways of expressing your love for Him.

Whatever we ask we receive from Him, because we keep His commandments and do those things that are pleasing in His sight. (1 John 3:22)

The Word of God clearly ties obedience to a genuine love for God. Born again believers will not find it wearying to live by God's Commandments. With all your sins washed away by the atoning death and precious blood of Jesus Christ, your obedience is rooted in His victorious life within you. Because you love Him so deeply for changing your life, you will actually go beyond the requirements of the Ten Commandments because you are now living according to the royal law of love. In other words, if I am walking in the love of Christ, I will not steal from you. I will not slander you behind your back. If I am walking in Jesus' love, then I will not covet your spouse, or your stuff. Another great verse is 1 John 3:22:

And whatever we ask we receive from Him, because we keep His commandments and do those things that are pleasing in His sight.

What is legalism?

Some are probably now asking the question, "How can you be certain that keeping the Ten Commandments is not legalism?" Again, we'll continue answering scriptural questions with scripture.

Here is the patience of the saints; here are those who keep the commandments of God and the faith of Jesus. (Revelation 14:12)

And they (The saints) overcame him (Satan) by the blood of the Lamb and by the word of their testimony, and they did not love their lives to the death. (Revelation 12:11)

So, what exactly is legalism? Legalism is when one tries to earn salvation by keeping rules, regulations, rituals, and doing good works instead of accepting salvation as a free gift. Saints, as described in the Word of God, are identified as having four characteristics:

- Obeying God.
- Trusting in the precious blood of Christ.
- Lovingly sharing their faith with others.

- Choosing to die rather than to sin.

These are the true qualities of a person who loves Christ and desires to follow Him.

Assurance of growth

How can one be sure that his or her intimate, personal relationship with Jesus will continue to grow?

Search the Scriptures. (John 5:39)

Pray without ceasing. (1 Thessalonians 5:17)

As you therefore have received Christ Jesus the Lord, so walk in Him. (Colossians 2:6)

I die daily. (1 Corinthians 15:31)

No personal relationship can grow or stay alive without open, honest communication. Times of prayer and Bible study are forms of communication with our Father God, and they are vitally essential in keeping your personal relationship with Him growing. The Bible is His "love letter" to you that you'll desire to read and feed into your spirit daily as supernatural nourishment. Conversing with the Father in prayer will deepen your devotion and open you up to a more thrilling and intimate knowledge of who He is and what He seeks to do in your life. You'll learn details of His incredible provision for your happiness. Equally important, you'll discover that your love for Jesus will also deepen as you share His love with others. As in other personal relationships, you'll need to remember, that the loss of love can turn a paradise into slavery. When one ceases to love the Lord, then religion will exist only as forced compliance to a set of restrictions.

It is imperative that once you've accepted Jesus as personal Savior and Lord, that you be baptized in water which lets everyone know about your life-changing relationship with Him. Water baptism is the outward sign and public profession to the church of the inward miracle of your reborn spirit in Christ.

We were buried with Him through baptism into death, that just as Christ was raised from the dead by the glory of the Father, even so we also should walk in newness of life... that the body of sin might be done away with, that we should no longer be slaves of sin. (Romans 6:4, 6)

I have betrothed you to one husband, that I may present you as a chaste virgin to Christ. (2 Corinthians 11:2)

Water Baptism symbolizes the significant components in the life of one who has accepted Jesus Christ:

- Death to sin.

- Birth to a new life in Christ.

- A spiritual "marriage" with Jesus for eternity. This spiritual union will grow stronger with time, as long as we continue in His love.

The Lord has promised to never forsake you (Psalm 55:22; Matthew 28:20 & Hebrews 13:5), and to provide for every need that could possibly develop in your lifetime (Matthew 6:25-34). Just as you received Him by faith, keep on trusting Him for every future need, and He will never let you down.

Anthony Sluzas

5

ISN'T THE CONCEPT OF OBEDIENCE REALLY JUST LEGALISM?

IT seems that many people feel it is okay to violate minor traffic laws or perhaps to cheat "a little" on their taxes, but God and His laws work much differently. God sees everything that we do, knows every thought, and He hears everything we say. He really does care about how we treat His law. While the Lord offers forgiveness for all our sins, it doesn't mean there aren't consequences for breaking God's law. Amazingly, some Christians say that any attempt to obey God's law amounts to "legalism" and yet Jesus said that if you really love God, you'll do what He asks. Okay then, is obedience really legalism? Continue reading, dear one. Eternal consequences are at stake.

Does God really care?

Does God really care about every minute detail of your life? Does He see all and take care of you personally?

You-Are-the-God-Who-Sees. (Genesis 16:13)

O Lord, You have searched me and known me. You know my sitting down and my rising up. You understand my thought afar off. You comprehend my path and my lying down, and are acquainted with all my ways. For there is not a word on my tongue, but behold, O Lord, You know it altogether. (Psalm 139:1-4).

But the very hairs of your head are all numbered. (Luke 12:7)

God knows you and every other human being on earth better than we know ourselves. He takes a personal interest in each and every individual and sees all that we do. Not one word, thought, or deed is hidden from Him.

Why obedience is important

Let's be very clear. Salvation and the kingdom of heaven are for those who obey the Lord's commands. God does not promise eternal life to those who merely make a profession of faith, or are church members, or are baptized but rather, to those who do His will, which is revealed in the Bible. Search the Word of God for His perfect will. It is your only safety. Bottom line: This obedience is only possible through a personal relationship with Jesus Christ (Acts 4:12).

Not everyone who says to Me, 'Lord, Lord,' shall enter the kingdom of heaven, but he who does the will of My Father in heaven. (Matthew 7:21)

If you want to enter into life, keep the commandments. (Matthew 19:17)

He became the author of eternal salvation to all who obey Him. (Hebrews 5:9)

Why exactly does Almighty God require obedience? Why is it necessary? It is because only one path leads to God's kingdom. All roads do not lead to the same place. The Word of God is our roadmap. It is the guidebook with all the instructions, warnings, and information on how to safely reach the kingdom of heaven. If we disregard any of God's Word, we will drift further and further away from God's Kingdom. The universe of God is of one law and order; including natural, moral, and spiritual. Breaking any of these laws has fixed consequences. If the Bible had not been given, people would have, sooner or later, discovered by trial and error that the great principles of the Author of life exist and are true. When ignored, they result in torment, sickness, and unhappiness of every kind. Thus, the words of the Bible are not merely advice that we can ignore without consequences. God's Word tells us what these consequences are and explains how to avoid them. A person cannot live any old way that he or she wishes and still become Christlike any more than a builder can ignore the blueprints for a house without running into big trouble. This is why the Lord God wants you to follow the blueprint of life—The Bible. There is simply no other way to true fulfillment in this life and in the next.

Because narrow is the gate and difficult is the way which leads to life, and there are few who find it. (Matthew 7:14)

He who sins against me wrongs his own soul; All those who hate me love death. (Proverbs 8:36)

And the Lord commanded us to observe all these statutes, to fear the Lord, our God, for our good always, that He might preserve us alive, as it is this day. (Deuteronomy 6:24)

The ultimate end of disobedience

Ever wonder why God permits such rampant disobedience all around us and why He allows it to even continue? Why not just destroy all the sin in the world and sinners right now? That would be the end of all of us. God will not destroy sin until everyone has been fully convinced of His justice, love, and mercy. All will finally realize that God, by asking for obedience, is not trying to force His will upon us, but rather is trying to keep us from hurting and destroying ourselves. You see, the problem of sin is not settled until even the most cynical and hardened sinners are convinced of God's love and confess that He is just. It just may take a major catastrophe to convince some, but the horrible results of sinful living will finally convince all that God is just and His judgments right.

Behold, the Lord comes with tens of thousands of His saints, to execute judgment on all, to convict all who are ungodly among them of all their ungodly deeds which they have committed in an ungodly way, and of all the harsh things which ungodly sinners have spoken against Him. (Jude vv. 14-15)

"As I live," says the Lord, "Every knee shall bow to Me, and every tongue shall confess to God." (Romans 14:11)

What will be the final end for those in rebellion and disobedient unto God and for having rejected the free gift of salvation through Jesus Christ? The rebellious and disobedient, including Satan, his angels, and demonic hordes, will all be cast into the lake which burns with fire. This being true, surely it is time to abandon all humanistic, unbelieving falderal regarding what is right or wrong. It is dangerous for us to depend on our own notions and feelings of right and wrong. Our only safety is depending on God's Word alone. His Word is truth.

God did not spare the angels who sinned, but cast them down to hell and delivered them into chains of darkness, to be reserved for judgment. (2 Peter 2:4)

All the wicked He will destroy. (Psalm 145:20)

In flaming fire taking vengeance on those who do not know God, and on those who do not obey the gospel of our Lord Jesus Christ. (2 Thessalonians 1:8).

Some have loudly argued saying it is impossible to obey God completely. The truth is that none of us can obey in our own power, but if you are a blood-bought, born again child of God, then through Jesus, we can and must obey. Satan, in order to make God's requests appear unreasonable, invented the falsehood that obedience is impossible. However, prayerfully look at the following verses...

With God all things are possible. (Matthew 19:26)

Thanks be to God who always leads us in triumph in Christ. (2 Corinthians 2:14)

He who abides in Me, and I in him, bears much fruit; for without Me you can do nothing. (John 15:5)

If you are willing and obedient, you shall eat the good of the land. (Isaiah 1:19)

What will be the destiny of one who willfully continues in rebellion and disobedience? God's Word leaves no room for doubt. The answer is sobering but true. When a man or woman knowingly rejects light and continues in disobedience, then eventually the light goes out, and that person is left in total darkness. A person who rejects Christ and disobeys God's truth receives a "strong delusion" to believe that falsehood is truth (2 Thessalonians 2:11). When this happens, he or she is lost for all eternity.

If we sin willfully after we have received the knowledge of the truth, there no longer remains a sacrifice for sins, but a certain fearful expectation of judgment, and fiery indignation which will devour the adversaries. (Hebrews 10:26-27)

Walk while you have the light, lest darkness overtake you; he who walks in darkness does not know where he is going. (John 12:35)

The most important things

As a pastor and evangelist, I've heard the following question more than a few times over the years and as silly as it sounds now as I put it to paper, they sincerely meant it. The question was, "Isn't love more important than obedience?" The simple answer? God's Word actually teaches that true love to God does not exist without obedience. A person cannot be truly obedient without genuine love and appreciation for God. No child will fully obey his parents unless he loves them, nor will he show love to Dad and Mom if he does not obey. True love and obedience are inextricably linked. When they separate, they will die.

Jesus answered and said to him, "If anyone loves Me, he will keep My word... He who does not love Me does not keep My words." (John 14:23-24)

For this is the love of God, that we keep His commandments. And His commandments are not burdensome. (1 John 5:3)

Genuine liberty in Christ Jesus means that we have been set free from sin because of the cross (Romans 6:18). Freedom comes only from obedience. Citizens who obey the laws of the land (and God's) have freedom. The rebellious and disobedient are caught and lose their freedom. Freedom without obedience is a false freedom; it is self-deception and authored by Satan. It leads to confusion and ultimately, anarchy. True Christian liberty means freedom from disobedience. Disobedience always hurts the individual and leads one into the cruel slavery of the wicked one.

If you abide in My word, you are My disciples indeed. And you shall know the truth, and the truth shall make you free... whoever commits sin is a slave of sin. (John 8:31-32,34)

God be thanked that though you were slaves of sin, yet you obeyed from the heart that form of doctrine to which you were delivered. And having been set free from sin, you became slaves of righteousness. (Romans 6:17-18)

So, shall I keep Your law continually forever and ever and I will walk at liberty, for I seek Your precepts. (Psalm 119:44-45).

Heeding to obedience

There are times the Holy Spirit will require a certain thing of each of us that will defy human logic or reason. It is best to obey and do exactly as He says, when He says it, how He says, and the way He says to do it. We must give God credit for being wise enough to require some things of us that we might not understand. Good children obey their parents even when the reasons for their commands are not clear. Simple faith and trust in God will cause us to believe that He knows what is best for us and that He will never lead us down the wrong path. It is utter folly for us, in our ignorance, to distrust God's leadership even when we don't fully understand all His reasons.

Please, obey the voice of the Lord... So it shall be well with you, and your soul shall live. (Jeremiah 38:20)

He who trusts in his own heart is a fool. (Proverbs 28:26)

It is better to trust in the Lord than to put confidence in man. (Psalm 118:8)

As the heavens are higher than the earth, so are My ways higher than your ways, and My thoughts than your thoughts. (Isaiah 55:9)

How unsearchable are His judgments and His ways past finding out! For who has known the mind of the Lord? (Romans 11:33-34)

I will lead them in paths they have not known. (Romans 11:33-34).

Satan is fully aware that all disobedience is sin. He knows that sin brings unhappiness, tragedy, alienation from God, and eventual destruction. In his hatred, he tries to lead every human being into disobedience. The enemy wants you to disobey God because he hates you and wants you to be forever lost. You must wake up, face the facts, and make right decisions. Disobey and be lost, or accept Christ, obey and be saved. Your decision regarding obedience is a decision regarding Christ. You cannot separate our Lord from truth because He says:

I am... the truth. (John 14:6)

Choose for yourselves this day whom you will serve. (Joshua 25:15).

He who sins is of the devil, for the devil has sinned from the beginning... In this the children of God and the children of the devil are manifest: Whoever does not practice righteousness is not of God. (1 John 3:8,10)

Satan... deceives the whole world. (Revelation 12:9)

Our Heavenly Father promises that just as He worked a miracle to bring us the new birth experience, He will also continue to work needed miracles in our lives as we gladly follow Him until we are safe in His kingdom.

He Who began a good work in you will complete it until the day of Jesus Christ. (Philippians 1:6)

6

COUNTERFEITS, FALSE RELIGIONS, AND SPIRITUALITY

IF a self-proclaimed guru, spiritual leader, or prophet suddenly came on the scene and began drawing crowds with dynamic messages, seemingly working astonishing "miracles," bringing down fire from the sky, and revealing your personal secrets—would you believe in him or her? Should you believe? Your eternal destiny just might be tied directly to your ability to discern between true and false prophets. Thus, it is very important to know what the Bible really says about what is solidly grounded in scripture and what is counterfeit.

The work of prophets

Are there true prophets in our day, New Testament times and in the last days? Absolutely there are. Yes, both men and women will prophesy in the last days (Joel 2:28-32).

And it shall come to pass in the last days, says God, that I will pour out of My Spirit on all flesh; your sons and your daughters shall prophesy, your young men shall see visions, your old men shall dream dreams. (Acts 2:17)

The Lord Jesus Christ placed the ministry gift of prophets in His church, along with four other ministry offices: apostles, evangelists, pastors, and teachers (Ephesians 4:7-11).

For the equipping of the saints for the work of ministry, for the edifying of the body of Christ. (Ephesians 4:12)

Our Lord gave all five gifts (ministry offices) for the equipping of the saints. The equipping of the Lord's last days church would not be possible if any of these five gifts is missing.

Throughout the pages of the Bible, the gift of prophesy was not limited only to men. In addition to many men who had the gift of prophesy, God also gave the gift to at least eight women: Anna (Luke 2:36-38); Miriam (Exodus 15:20); Deborah (Judges 4:4); Huldah (2 Kings 22:14); and the four daughters of Philip, the evangelist (Acts 21:8-9). These gifts will remain until God's people are all unified, mature believers—which, of course, will be at the end of time "till we all come to the unity of the faith and of the knowledge of the Son of God, to a perfect man, to the measure of the stature of the fullness of Christ" (Ephesians 4:13).

Prophets do not express their own private opinions in spiritual matters. Their thoughts come from the Lord Jesus Christ, through the Holy Spirit.

Prophecy never came by the will of man, but holy men of God spoke as they were moved by the Holy Spirit. (2 Peter 1:21)

God speaks to prophets in three different ways; dreams, visions, and face-to-face. The Holy Spirit gives us the methods by which He speaks to the prophet in Numbers 12:6,8:

If there is a prophet among you, I, the Lord, make Myself known to him in a vision; I speak to him in a dream... I speak with him face-to-face.

Discerning true and false prophets

The following six Bible points provide the physical evidence of a true prophet. Not all of these six always appear together.

The vision of a prophet may indeed be genuine without manifesting all six evidence at once.

- A true prophet may lose physical strength when ministering (Daniel 10:8).

- He or she may receive supernatural strength (Daniel 10:18-19).

- No breath in the body (Daniel 10:17).

- Able to speak (Daniel 10:16).

- May not be aware of earthly surroundings in the moment (Daniel 10:5-8; 2 Corinthians 12:2-4).

- Eyes will be open (Numbers 24:4).

If miracles are wrought by the hands of a prophet, is that proof positive that he or she is of God? Not necessarily. In some cases, "they are spirits of demons, performing lying signs" (Revelation 16:14). Satan and his emissaries also have power to work lying signs and miracles (Deuteronomy 13:1-5; Revelation 13:13-14). Jesus warns us that in the perilous last days:

False 'christs' and false prophets will rise and show great signs and wonders to deceive, if possible, even the elect. (Matthew 24:24)

The Lord warns us of false 'christs' and false prophets who will be so cunning and convincing as to deceive all except the very elect of God. The Bible intimates billions will be deceived and eternally lost.

How does one determine if a prophet is true or false? We must test their teachings and conduct by the Word of God. If their teachings and behavior deviate from Scripture, they are false and "there is no light in them." Isaiah 8:20 tells us:

To the law and to the testimony! If they do not speak according to this word, it is because there is no light in them.

Are there specific kinds of false prophets specifically identified and condemned within the pages of the Bible? Yes, there certainly are. Deuteronomy 18:10-12 and Revelation 21:8 speak against the following types of false prophets:

- Soothsayers: Fortune-tellers.

- Sorcerers: Individuals who are believed to have magical powers or the ability to perform magical feats. A sorcerer is one who has learned these different abilities from another, perceived to be a master in their field.

- Mediums: Individuals who claim to communicate and channel (act as a host) for the spirits of the deceased. Mediums are also known as "spiritists" in modern times.

- Those who practice witchcraft: Also known as witches. These are individuals interested in developing the ability to engage with supernatural powers and do so by casting spells, using different methods of divination (ways to tell the future through various spirits), or worshiping or somehow engaging with nature.

- Those who interpret omens: Individuals who use different charms, natural methods, or in order to read "signs" about the future.

- Female or male psychics: Often identified as witches, soothsayers, or mediums in the Bible, a psychic is someone who is believed to perceive things beyond the natural senses. Psychics may perform magic feats as believed to do so by the senses (such as telepathy or future predictions), communicate with the dead (such as a medium) use aids such as tarot cards or crystals (such as in magic), or engage in paranormal investigations (such as with "ghost hunters").

Most of these false prophets claim to have contact with spirits of the dead. The Bible clearly states that the dead cannot be contacted by the living. Those supposed "spirits of the dead" are in reality, what the Bible calls, "familiar spirits." They literally are demon spirits that mimic and impersonate human beings that were once alive on earth (Leviticus 19:31; 20:6 & Revelation 16:13-14). Crystal balls, Ouija boards, palm reading, astrology, reading tea leaves, and conjuring and talking with spirits of the "dead" are not God's ways of communicating with people. The Bible plainly teaches and warns that all such things are an abomination unto God (Deuteronomy 18:12). Even worse, those who continue to be involved will be shut out of the Kingdom (Galatians 5:19-21; Revelation 21:8; 22:14-15).

<u>The work of a true prophet</u>

The work of a true prophet of God is primarily to serve, bless, and edify the church. The Word of God is clear. Although a prophet's message may sometimes edify the general public, the primary purpose of prophecy is to serve the church:

Prophesying is not for unbelievers but for those who believe. (1 Corinthians 14:22).

In the Epistle of 1 Corinthians 12:1-18, the Apostle Paul likens the gifts that Jesus gave the church to parts of the human body. What part of the body best represents the gift of prophecy? Since a prophet was originally called a seer (one who can see into the future), the eyes would best represent the gift of prophecy.

Formerly in Israel, when a man went to inquire of God, he spoke thus: 'Come, let us go to the seer'; for he who is now called a prophet was formerly called a seer. (1 Samuel 9:9)

It's been said that prophecy would be considered the eyes of the church. A church without the gift of prophecy would be considered blind.

They are blind leaders of the blind. And if the blind leads the blind, both will fall into a ditch. (Matthew 15:14)

The Bible plainly teaches that God's end time church will "come short in no gift," which means it must have all of the gifts: apostles, prophets, evangelists, pastors, teachers. This includes the gift of prophecy (1 Corinthians 1:5-8).

Revelation 12:17 points out that the church of the last days will "have the testimony of Jesus Christ." Revelation 19:10 says:

The testimony of Jesus is the spirit of prophecy.

The "testimony of Jesus" means the words of a prophet are from Jesus. We are to regard the words of a true prophet as a special and direct message from the Lord to us (Revelation 1:1; Amos 3:7). Any mocking or bringing reproach upon a true prophet is very dangerous. It is the same as bringing reproach upon Jesus, who sends and guides them. It's no wonder God warns:

Do My prophets no harm. (Psalm 105:15)

As we close out this chapter, we leave you with the Bible's qualifications for a true prophet. These qualifications are as follows:

- Live a godly life (Matthew 7:15-20).

- Be called to service by God (Isaiah 6:1-10; Jeremiah 1:5-10; Amos 7:14-15).

- Speak and write in harmony with the Bible (Isaiah 8:19-20).

- Predicts events that come true (Deuteronomy 18:20-22).

- Will have visions (Numbers 12:6).

The Apostle Paul gives a three-point command in regard to a prophet and prophecy.:

Do not despise prophecies. Test all things; hold fast what is good. (1 Thessalonians 5:20-21)

The Lord Jesus Christ counted the rejection of a true prophet as rejecting the will of God (Luke 7:28-30). Further, He stated that spiritual prosperity hinges upon believing His prophets (2 Chronicles 20:20).

You will deepen in love for Jesus, experience a vibrant new excitement for Scripture, and gain a fresh understanding of Bible prophecies when you listen to those with a genuine gift of prophecy. Remember, Jesus said He would bless His church in the last days with helpful prophetic messages. This is exciting! He is doing everything heaven can do for His people in the last days. The Lord intends to save His people and take them into the eternal heavenly kingdom. Those who faithfully follow Him are guaranteed entrance to heaven (Matthew 19:27-29). That's good news!

Anthony Sluzas

7

MARRIAGE BY-THE-BOOK

YES, it happens all over the world on a daily basis: the tragedy of divorce; unfaithfulness, broken promises, bitterness, confused and scarred children. Don't let this happen to your family. Whether your marriage is going through storms or experiencing relative bliss—or even if you're not yet married but are considering it—the Bible offers proven guidance from the Holy Spirit to help your marriage last. It is advice directly from God, the One who created and ordained marriage. If you've tried everything else, why not give the God of the universe a chance? Here are some important Bible keys for a happier marriage.

Establish your own home built on the Rock of Jesus Christ

Therefore, a man shall leave his father and mother and be joined to his wife, and they shall become one flesh. (Genesis 2:24).

God's principle is that a married couple should move out of their parents' homes and establish their own, even if finances require something modest, such as a one-room apartment. A husband and wife should decide this together, as one, and remain firm even is someone opposes them. Many marriages would be improved if this principle were carefully followed.

Continue your courtship

Above all things have fervent love for one another, for love will cover a multitude of sins. (1 Peter 4:8)

Her husband... praises her. (Proverbs 31:28)

She who is married cares... how she may please her husband. (1 Corinthians 7:34)

Be kindly affectionate to one another... in honor giving preference to one another. (Romans 12:10)

Continue—or revive—your courtship process well into your married life. Successful marriages don't just happen; they must be developed. Don't take one another for granted, or the resulting monotony could harm your marriage. Keep your love for one another growing by expressing it to each other; otherwise, love might fade and you could drift apart. Love and happiness are not found by seeking them for yourself, but rather by generously giving them to others. So, spend as much time as possible doing things together. Learn to greet each other with enthusiasm. Relax, visit, sightsee, and eat together. Don't overlook the little courtesies, encouragements, and affectionate acts. Surprise each other with gifts or favors. Try to "out-love" your partner. Don't try to take more out of your marriage than you put into it. Lack of love is the biggest destroyer of marriage.

Remember that God joined you together in marriage

For this reason, a man shall leave his father and mother and be joined to his wife, and the two shall become one flesh'? So then, they are no longer two but one flesh. Therefore, what God has joined together, let not man separate. (Matthew 19:5-6)

Has love nearly disappeared from your home? While the devil wants to tear apart your marriage by tempting you to give up, don't forget that God Himself joined you together in marriage, and He desires that you stay together and be happy. He will bring happiness and love into your lives if you will obey His divine commandments.

With God, all things are possible. (Matthew 19:26)

Don't despair. God's Spirit can change your heart and your spouse's heart if you will ask and let Him.

<u>Guard your thoughts. Guard your heart</u>

As he thinks in his heart, so is he. (Proverbs 28:7)

You shall not covet your neighbor's wife. (Exodus 20:17)

Keep your heart with all diligence, for out of it spring the issues of life. (Proverbs 4:23)

Whatever things are true... noble... just... pure... lovely... of good report... meditate on these things. (Philippians 4:8)

Wrong thinking can profoundly harm your marriage. The evil one will tempt you with thoughts like, "Our marriage was a mistake." "She doesn't understand me." "I can't take much more of this." "We can always divorce if necessary." "I'll go home to mother," or, "He smiled at that woman." This kind of thinking is dangerous, because your thoughts ultimately govern your actions. Avoid seeing, saying, reading, or hearing anything that—or anything associated with anyone who—suggests being unfaithful. Uncontrolled thoughts are like leaving your vehicle in neutral on a steep hill; the results could be disastrous.

<u>Here's an oldie, but goodie: Never go to bed angry</u>

Do not the sun go down on your wrath. (Ephesians 4:26)

Confess your trespasses to one another. (James 5:16)

Forgetting those things which are behind. (Philippians 3:13)

Be kind to one another, tenderhearted, forgiving one another, even as God in Christ forgave you. (Philippians 4:32)

Remaining angry over hurts and grievances – whether large or small – can be dangerous to a relationship. Unless addressed in a timely manner, even little problems can become set in your mind as convictions and can adversely affect your outlook on life. This is why God said to let your anger cool down before going to bed. Be big enough to forgive and to say, "I'm sorry." After all, not one of us is perfect, and both of you are on the same team, so be gracious enough to admit a mistake when you make it. Besides, making up is a very pleasant experience, with unusual powers to draw marriage partners closer together. It works!

Most important of all: Keep Christ at the center of your home

Unless the Lord builds the house, they labor in vain who build it. (Psalm 127:1)

In all your ways acknowledge Him, and He shall direct your paths. (Proverbs 3:6)

And the peace of God, which surpasses all understanding, will guard your hearts and minds through Christ Jesus. (Philippians 4:7)

Keeping Christ at the center of your marriage and home is the greatest principle, because it is the only one that enables all the others. The vital ingredient of happiness in the home is not in diplomacy, strategy, or our efforts to overcome problems, but rather in a union with Christ. Hearts filled with the love of Jesus will not be far apart for long. With Christ in the home, a marriage has a greater chance at being successful. Jesus can wash away bitterness and disappointment and restore love and happiness.

Pray together

Watch and pray, lest you enter into temptation. The spirit indeed is willing, but the flesh is weak. (Matthew 26:41)

Pray for one another. (James 5:16)

If any of you lacks wisdom, let him ask of God, who gives to

all liberally and without reproach, and it will be given to him liberally. (James 1:5)

Pray with one another! This is a wonderful activity that will help your marriage succeed beyond your wildest dreams. Kneel before God and ask Him for true love for one another, for forgiveness, for strength, for wisdom—for the solutions to problems. God will answer. You won't be automatically cured of every fault, but God will have greater access to change your heart and actions.

<u>Agree that divorce is not the answer</u>

What God has joined together, let not man separate. (Matthew 19:6)

Whoever divorces his wife, except for sexual immorality, and marries another, commits adultery; and whoever marries her who is divorced commits adultery. (Matthew 19:9)

The woman who has a husband is bound by the law to her husband as long as he lives. (Romans 7:2).

The Bible says that the ties of marriage are meant to be unbreakable. Divorce is allowed only in cases of adultery or when an unbeliever abandons a believing spouse. But even then, it is not demanded. Forgiveness is always better than divorce, even in the case of unfaithfulness. When God ordained the first marriage in Eden, He designed it for life. Thus, marriage vows are among the most solemn and binding. But remember, God meant for marriage to elevate our lives and meet our needs in every way. Harboring thoughts of divorce will tend to destroy your marriage. Divorce is always destructive and is almost never a solution to the problem; instead, it usually creates greater problems—financial troubles, grieving children, etc. You will likely carry your emotional baggage into a future relationship with the same results.

<u>Keep the family circle closed securely</u>

You shall not commit adultery. (Exodus 20:14)

The heart of her husband safely trusts her... She does him good and not evil all the days of her life. (Proverbs 31:11-12)

The Lord has been the witness between you and the wife of your youth, with whom you have dealt treacherously. (Malachi 2:14)

Keep you from the evil woman... Do not lust after her beauty in your heart, nor let her allure you with her eyelids. Can a man take fire to his bosom, and his clothes not be burned? So is he who goes in to his neighbor's wife; whoever touches her shall not be innocent. (Proverbs 6:24, 25, 27, 29)

Private family matters should never be shared with others outside your home; not even parents. Another person outside the marriage to sympathize with or listen to complaints can be used by the devil to estrange the hearts of a husband and wife. Solve your private home problems privately. No one else, except a minister or a marriage counselor, should be involved. Always be truthful with each other and never keep secrets. Avoid telling jokes at the expense of your spouse's feelings, and vigorously defend each other. Adultery will always hurt you and everyone else in your family. God, who knows your mind, body, and feelings, said:

You shall not commit adultery. (Exodus 20:14)

If flirtations have already begun, break them off immediately—or shadows could settle over your life that cannot be easily lifted.

Make it a daily goal to experience the love of God

Love suffers long and is kind; love does not envy; love does not parade itself, is not puffed up; does not behave rudely, does not seek its own, is not provoked, thinks no evil; does not rejoice in iniquity, but rejoices in the truth; bears all things, believes all things, hopes all things, endures all things. (1 Corinthians 13:4-7)

The above portion of Scripture is one of God's greatest descriptions of love. Read it. Speak it. Feed on it again and again. Have you made these words part of your marriage experience? True love is not mere sentimental impulse, but rather a quality decision and holy principle that involves every aspect of your married life. With true love, your marriage stands a far greater chance for success; without it, a marriage will likely fall apart in short order.

Remember that negativity, nagging, and a critical spirit can destroy love

Husbands, love your wives and do not be bitter toward them. (Colossians 3:19)

Better to dwell in the wilderness than with a contentious and angry woman. (Proverbs 21:19)

A continual dripping on a very rainy day and a contentious woman are alike. (Proverbs 27:15)

And why do you look at the speck in your brother's eye, but do not consider the plank in your own eye? (Matthew 7:3)

Love suffers long and is kind; love does not envy; love does not parade itself. (1 Corinthians 13:4)

Stop finding fault in your partner

Your spouse might lack much, but your criticism won't help. Expecting perfection will bring bitterness to you and your spouse. Ask the Lord to help you overlook their faults and hunt for the good things. Don't try to reform, control, or compel your partner – you will destroy love. Only God can change people. A sense of humor, a cheerful heart, kindness, patience, and affection will banish many of your marriage problems. A Pastor once told a disgruntled husband, "Try to make your spouse happy rather than good, and the good will likely take care of itself. The secret of a successful marriage lies not in having the right partner, but in being the right partner."

Do not overdo or go overboard in anything, but be temperate

Overdoing will ruin your marriage, and so will underdoing. Time with God, love, work, rest, exercise, recreation, meals, and social contact must be balanced in a marriage or something will snap. Too much work and a lack of rest, proper food and exercise can lead a person to be critical, intolerant, and negative. The Bible also recommends a temperate sex life (1 Corinthians 7:3-6) because degrading and intemperate sex acts can destroy love and respect for one another. Social contact with others is essential because true happiness won't be found in isolation. We must team to laugh and enjoy wholesome, good times. Being serious all the time is dangerous. Overdoing or underdoing in anything weakens the mind, body, conscience, and the ability to love and respect one another. Don't let intemperance damage your marriage.

Everyone who competes for the prize is temperate in all things. (1 Corinthians 9:25)

Love... does not seek its own [selfish advantage]. (1 Corinthians 13:4-5).

Whether you eat or drink, or whatever you do, do all to the glory of God. (1 Corinthians 10:31)

I discipline my body and bring it into subjection. (1 Corinthians 9:27)

If anyone will not work, neither shall he eat. (2 Thessalonians 3:10)

Marriage is honorable among all, and the bed undefiled. (Hebrews 13:4)

Do not let sin reign in your mortal body, that you should obey it in its lusts and do not present your members as instruments of unrighteousness to sin. (Romans 6:12-13)

Respect one another's personal rights and privacies

Each spouse has God-given right certain personal privacies.

Do not tamper with each other's personal effects, such as a wallet or purse, personal email, and other private property, unless given permission. The right to privacy and quietude when preoccupied should be respected. Your husband or wife even has a right to be wrong sometimes, and is entitled to a bad day without being given the third degree about this or that. Marriage partners do not own each other and should never try to force personality changes. Confidence and trust in one another are essential for happiness, so don't check up on each other constantly. Spend less time trying to "figure out" your spouse and more time trying to please her or him. Doing this can work wonders.

Love suffers long and is kind... Love does not envy... does not behave rudely, does not seek its own [in selfishness] ... does not rejoice in iniquity... believes all things, hopes all things, endures all things. (1 Corinthians 13:4-7)

Be kindly affectionate to one another with brotherly love, in honor giving preference to one another. (Romans 12:10)

<u>On a very practical side: be clean, modest, orderly, and dutiful</u>

Carelessness, laziness, and disorder can be used by the enemy to destroy your respect and affection for one another and thus, seriously harm your marriage. Modest attire and clean, well-groomed bodies are important for both a husband and wife. Both partners should take care to create a home environment that is clean and orderly, as this will help bring peace and calmness. A lazy, shiftless spouse who does not contribute to the household is a disadvantage to the family and is displeasing to God. Everything done for one another should be done with care and respect. Carelessness in these seemingly small matters has caused discord and division in countless homes.

In like manner also, that the women adorn themselves in modest apparel. (1 Timothy 2:9)

She... willingly works with her hands... She also rises while it is yet night, and provides food for her household... She watches over the ways of her household, and does not eat the bread of idleness. (Proverbs 31:13, 15, 27)

Be clean. (Isaiah 52:11)

If anyone does not provide for his own, and especially for those of his household, he has denied the faith and is worse than an unbeliever. (1 Timothy 5:8)

Do not become sluggish [lazy]. (Hebrews 6:12).

Determine to speak softly and kindly

Always endeavor to speak softly and kindly to your spouse, even during heated disputes. Decisions made when angry, tired, or discouraged are unreliable anyway, so it's best to relax and let anger cool down before speaking. And when you do speak, let it always be calmly and lovingly. Harsh or angry words can crush your spouse's spirit and desire to please you.

A soft answer turns away wrath, but a harsh word stirs up anger. (Proverbs 15:1)

Live joyfully with the wife whom you love. (Ecclesiastes 9:9).

When I became a man, I put away childish things. (1 Corinthians 13:11)

Be reasonable and flexible in financial affairs

Household income should be shared in a marriage, with each partner having the right to spend a certain portion as desired and according to the agreed upon family budget. Separate bank accounts are the decision of each couple, but separate accounts often tend to remove the opportunity to deepen trust, which is vital for a healthy marriage. Money management is supposed to be a team effort. Both partners should be involved, but one should take the ultimate responsibility. Money management roles should be determined by personal abilities and preferences.

Love does not envy [is not possessive] ... does not behave rudely, does not seek its own [selfish advantage]. (1

Corinthians 13:4-5)

God loves a cheerful giver. (2 Corinthians 9:7)

<u>Talk things over freely and openly with one another</u>

Few things will strengthen your marriage more than praying together in order to seek God's will, and having open discussions on major decisions. Changing a job, purchasing something expensive, and other major life decisions should involve both husband and wife—and differing opinions should be respected. Talking things over together and earnest prayer will avoid many blunders that could greatly weaken your marriage (see Ephesians 5:22-25).

Love suffers long and is kind; love does not envy; love does not parade itself, is not puffed up. (1 Corinthians 13:4)

He who disdains instruction despises his own soul. (Proverbs 15:32)

Do you see a man wise in his own eyes? There is more hope for a fool than for him. (Proverbs 26:12)

Anthony Sluzas

8
DO YOU REALLY TRUST GOD?

WELL, do you trust God? The truth is, a lot of people might say yes, but they're actions betray their positive affirmations. And worse, because they don't trust Him, they might actually steal from Him. "Oh, come on!" you say, "No one would steal from God." However, God's shocking message to His people is:

You have robbed Me. (Malachi 3:8)

Real financial records worldwide prove that billions of people steal from God, and as incredible as it may seem, they use that stolen money to subsidize their own reckless spending. Yet many are unaware of their larceny, and in this chapter, we'll show you how to avoid that same mistake and how to prosper through genuine faith in God.

The tithe

According to the Bible, what portion of our income belongs to God? The tithe belongs to the Lord.

All the tithe of the land... is the Lord's. (Leviticus 27:30)

The tithe is one-tenth of a person's income. The word "tithe" literally means "tenth." The tithe belongs to God. It is His. We have no right to keep it. When we tithe, we are not presenting a gift; we are simply returning to God what is already His. Unless we are returning one-tenth of our income to God, we are not tithing.

Where does the Lord ask His people to bring the tithe?

Bring all the tithes into the storehouse. (Malachi 3:10)

What is the Lord's "storehouse?"

Then all Judah brought the tithe of the grain and the new wine and the oil to the storehouse. (Nehemiah 13:12)

In Malachi 3:10, God refers to the storehouse as "My house," which means His temple, or church. Nehemiah 13:12-13, further points out that the tithe is to be brought to the temple treasury, which is God's storehouse. Other texts that refer to the storehouse as the temple treasuries, or chambers, include 1 Chronicles 9:26; 2 Chronicles 31:11-12 and Nehemiah 10:37-38. In Old Testament times, God's people brought 10 percent of all their increase – including crops and animals – to the storehouse.

More than a few people have claimed that tithing was part of Moses' system of rites and ceremonies that ended at the Cross. Is this true? Let's answer that with actual scripture.

And he [Abram] gave him a tithe of all. (Genesis 14:20)

In Genesis 28:22, Jacob said:

Of all that You give me I will surely give a tenth to You.

These passages reveal that both Abraham and Jacob, who lived long before Moses' day, tithed their income. We can therefore conclude that God's plan of tithing is not limited to Moses' law and applies to all people of all times. Not convinced? Keep reading.

For what was the tithe used in Old Testament days? The tithe in the Old Covenant was used for the income of the priests. The tribe of Levi (the priests) received no portion of land for crop growing and business operations, while the other tribes did. The Levites worked full time, taking care of the temple, and ministering to God's people. So, God's plan was for tithes to support the priests and their families.

Behold, I have given the children of Levi all the tithes in Israel as an inheritance in return for the work which they perform, the work of the tabernacle of meeting. (Numbers 18:21)

Did God change His plan for tithe usage in New Testament days? The answer is no. God continued it, and today His plan is for the tithe to be used to support those who work solely in gospel ministry. If everyone obeyed God, and tithed and the tithes were used strictly for the support of gospel workers, there would be more than enough money to reach the entire world very quickly with God's end-time gospel message.

Do you not know that those who minister the holy things eat of the things of the temple, and those who serve at the altar partake of the offerings of the altar? Even so the Lord has commanded that those who preach the gospel should live from the gospel. (1 Corinthians 9:13-14)

Didn't Jesus abolish the plan of tithing? On the contrary, Jesus endorsed and reaffirmed the tithe. He rebuked the Jews for omitting the more important matters of the law – justice, mercy, faith – even though they were meticulous tithers. He then plainly told them they should continue tithing but also be just and merciful and faithful.

Woe to you, scribes and Pharisees, hypocrites! For you pay tithes of mint and anise and cumin, and have neglected the weightier matters of the law: justice and mercy and faith. These you ought to have done, without leaving the others undone. (Matthew 23:23).

What startling offer does God make to people who feel uncertain about tithing? He says, "Try Me now" and see that I will give you such a blessing that it will be too overwhelming to receive! This is the only time in the Bible that God makes such a proposal. He is saying, "Give it a try. It will work. I promise you." Hundreds of thousands of tithers the world over will gladly testify to the truth of God's tithing promise. They have all learned the truth of these words, "You can't out-give God."

So, when we tithe, who really receives our money?

Here mortal men receive tithes, but there he receives them. (Hebrews 7:8)

Jesus, our heavenly High Priest, receives our tithes. When you return God's tithe, you make Him a partner in absolutely everything you undertake. What a fantastic, blessed privilege. God and you – partners! With our Father as a partner, you have everything to gain and nothing to lose. However, it is a dangerous proposition to take God's own money, which He has earmarked for saving souls, and use it for our own personal budgets and fun.

Offerings

In addition to the tithe, which belongs to God, what else does God ask of His people? Our Lord asks us to give offerings for His work as an expression of our love for Him and our thanksgiving for His blessings.

Bring an offering, and come into His courts. (Psalm 96:8)

How much shall I give to God in offerings? The Bible does not specify a set amount for offerings. Each person decides, as God impresses, how much to give and then gives it cheerfully.

So, let each one give as he purposes in his heart, not grudgingly or of necessity; for God loves a cheerful giver. (2 Corinthians 9:7).

It's often been said that "you can give without loving, but you cannot love without giving." Yes, loving is all about giving. Let's look at additional Bible principles that our Lord shares with us regarding giving:

- Our first priority should be to give ourselves to the Lord (2 Corinthians 8:5).

- We should give God our very best (Proverbs 3:9).

- God blesses the generous giver (Proverbs 11:24-25).

- It is more blessed to give than to receive (Acts 20:35).

- When cheap and miserly, we are not rightly using our God-given blessings (Luke 12:16-21).

- God always returns more than we give (Luke 6:38).

- We should give in proportion to how God has prospered and blessed us (1 Corinthians 16:2).

- We should give as we are able (Deuteronomy 16:17).

- We return the tithe (one-tenth) to God, to whom it already belongs. We also give offerings, which are voluntary and should be given joyously.

What does the Lord own? According to His Word, He owns:

- All the silver and gold in the world (Haggai 2:8).

- The earth and all its people (Psalm 24:1).

- The world and everything in it (Psalm 24:1).

God permits people to use and steward His great riches. He also gives them the wisdom and power to prosper and yes, accumulate wealth (Deuteronomy 8:18). In return for furnishing everything unto us, all that God asks is that we return to Him the tithe (ten percent) of our increase as our acknowledgement of His great investment in our business affairs and careers – as well as offerings for an expression of our love and gratitude.

How does God view those who do not return His tithe and give offerings? He bluntly refers to them as robbers. Can you imagine people stealing from God?

Will a man rob God? Yet you have robbed Me! But you say, 'In what way have we robbed You?' In tithes and offerings. (Malachi 3:8)

What does God say will happen to those who knowingly continue to rob Him in tithes and offerings? A curse will rest upon their finances and the things they set their hands to do.

You are cursed with a curse, for you have robbed Me. (Malachi 3:9)

God warns us against the sin of covetousness. Why is covetousness dangerous? Because our hearts follow our investments. If our focus is on accumulating more and more money, our hearts become covetous, discontented, and proud. However, if our focus is on sharing, on helping others, and God's kingdom work, then our hearts will become caring, loving, giving, and humble. Covetousness is one of the terrible sins of the last days that will shut people out of heaven (2 Timothy 3:1-7).

    How does the Lord Jesus Himself feel when we rob Him of tithes and offerings? He certainly feels much as parents do when a child steals money from them. The money itself is not the main issue. It is the child's lack of integrity, love, and trust that is deeply disappointing.

Therefore, I was angry with that generation, and said, "They always go astray in their heart, and have not known My ways." (Hebrews 3:10)

There's a very uplifting passage written by the Apostle Paul in 1 Corinthians chapter 8 regarding the stewardship of the believers in Macedonia. Paul had written to the churches in Macedonia asking them to lay aside funds for God's people in Jerusalem, who were suffering through an extended famine. He told them he would pick up these gifts when he came to their cities on his next visit. The thrilling response from the churches in Macedonia described in chapter 8 is quite heartening:

- As a first step, they rededicated their lives to Jesus Christ (v. 5).

- Though in "deep poverty" themselves, they gave "beyond their ability" to give (vv. 2-3).

- They urged Paul to come back and pick up their gifts (v. 4).

- Their gifts followed the sacrificial example of Jesus (v. 9).

The love of God's people in Macedonia caused them to give liberally to the famine-stricken Christians in Jerusalem. If we truly love Jesus, giving sacrificially for His work will never be a burden but a glorious privilege that we will perform with great joy.

Billy Graham once said, "Show me your checkbook and I'll show you what's really important to you." What does our heavenly Father promise to do for those who are faithful in returning tithes and giving offerings? God promises to prosper His faithful financial stewards, and they will be a blessing to those around them.

Consider just some of the following ways God blesses His faithful children:

- God promises that your nine-tenths will go further with His blessing than your total income would go without it. If you doubt this, ask any faithful tither!

- Blessings are not always financial. They may include health, peace of mind, answered prayer, protection, a close-knit and loving family, added physical strength, ability to make wise decisions, a spirit of gratitude, a closer walk with Jesus, success in soul-winning, an older vehicle kept running longer than one would think it should operate, etc.

- The Lord becomes your partner in everything. No one except God could ever structure a plan so utterly amazing.

What do you say? Are you willing and obedient to take God at His Word by returning His tithe to Him as well as offerings to bless others? Loved one, you can't afford not to tithe, and the blessings God will return to you for your obedience and faithfulness are out of this world!

9

LOVE THAT TRANSFORMS

IT'S often been said that being in love changes everything! When a young lady had to read a very large and cumbersome book for her college English literature course, she found it very boring and could barely stay focused while reading it. Then one day, she met a handsome young professor on campus, and they quickly fell in love. Soon after, she realized her beloved was the author of the book she had struggled with. That night, she stayed awake and devoured the entire book, exclaiming, "Oh my goodness, this is the best book I've ever read!" So, what changed her perspective? Love did! Likewise, many today find Scripture boring, unappealing, and even oppressive. But all that changes when you fall in love with its Author.

Love that changes us

Who is the Author of Scripture? Every book in the Bible points to the Lord Jesus Christ—even the entirety of the Old Testament books. Jesus created the world (John 1:1-3, 14; Colossians 1:13-17), wrote the Ten Commandments (Nehemiah 9:6, 13), was the God of the Israelites (1 Corinthians 10:1-4), and guided the writings of the prophets (1 Peter 1:10-11). So, our Lord Jesus Christ is the Author of Scripture.

The prophets have inquired and searched carefully, who prophesied of the grace that would come to you, searching what, or what manner of time, the Spirit of Christ who was in them was indicating when He testified beforehand the sufferings of Christ and the glories that would follow. (1 Peter 1:10-11)

What is Jesus' attitude toward the people of this earth? Jesus loves us all with an unfailing love that passes all understanding.

For God so loved the world that He gave His only begotten Son, that whoever believes in Him should not perish but have everlasting life. For God did not send His Son into the world to condemn the world, but that the world through Him might be saved. (John 3:16-17)

We love Him because He loved us enough to die for us – while we were yet His enemies.

While we were still sinners, Christ died for us. (Romans 5:8)

We love Him because He first loved us. (1 John 4:19)

A good and godly marriage is compared to the Church within the pages of the New Testament. In what respects are a solid marriage and the Christian life similar? In a truly good marriage, certain things are imperative, such as faithfulness to one's spouse. Other things may not seem major, but if they please a spouse, they are necessary. If they displease, they should be discontinued. It is very similar with the Christian life. The commands of Jesus are imperative. But in Scripture, Jesus has also outlined for us principles of conduct that please Him. As in a good marriage, Christians will find it a joy to do things that make Jesus, the One we love, happy. We will also consciously avoid things that displease Him.

Whatever we ask we receive from Him, because we keep His commandments and do those things that are pleasing in His sight. (1 John 3:22)

What does Jesus say are the results of doing the things that please Him? The evil one claims that to follow Christian principles is drab, dull, demeaning, and legalistic. But Jesus says that following Him and His commands brings fullness of joy—and a more abundant life (John 10:10). Believing the devil's lies brings conflict, heartache and deprives people of life that is "really living."

If you keep My commandments, you will abide in My love, just as I have kept My Father's commandments and abide in His love. These things I have spoken to you, that My joy may remain in you, and that your joy may be full. (John 15:10-11)

Why does Jesus give us very relevant and specific principles for Christian living? Because they:

- "Are for our good always" (Deuteronomy 6:24). As good parents teach good principles to their children, so Jesus teaches good principles to His children.

- Set for us a safeguard from sin (Psalm 119:11). Jesus' principles protect us from entering the danger zones of Satan and sin.

- Show us how to follow in Christ's footsteps (1 Peter 2:21).

- Bring us true joy (John 13:17).

- Give us an opportunity to express our love for Him (John 15:10).

- Help us be a good example to others (1 Corinthians 10:31-33; Matthew 5:16).

<u>Do not be conformed to this world</u>

According to Jesus, how should Christians relate to the evil all around us and worldliness? His commands and counsels are clear and specific. Don't love the world or the things of this world. This includes the lust of the flesh, the lust of the eyes, and the pride of life (1 John 2:16). All sin falls into one or more of these categories. To be sure, Satan uses these avenues to lure us into the love of the world. When we begin to love the world, we become an enemy of God (1 John 2:15-16; James 4:4). We must keep ourselves unspotted from the world (James 1:27).

What urgent warning does God give us regarding this present world? Jesus warns:

Do not be conformed to this world. (Romans 12:2)

The devil is not neutral. He presses every Christian constantly. Through Jesus (Philippians 4:13), we must firmly resist the devil's suggestions, and he will flee from us (James 4:7). The minute we permit the pressure or "squeezing" of any other factor to influence our conduct, we, perhaps imperceptibly, begin slipping into apostasy. Christian behavior is not to be decided by feelings and the conduct of the majority, but by Jesus' words alone.

Why do we as followers of Jesus Christ need to guard our thoughts?

As a man thinks in his heart, so is he. (Proverbs 23:7)

We must guard our thoughts because thoughts dictate our behavior. God wants to help us bring "every thought into captivity to the obedience of Christ" (2 Corinthians 10:5). At the same time, Satan desperately wants to bring "the world" into our thoughts. He can do this only through our five senses—especially sight and hearing. He presses his sights and sounds upon us and unless we consistently refuse what he offers, he will direct us into the broad way that leads to destruction. The Bible is clear: We become like the things we repeatedly see, hear, and worship (2 Corinthians 3:18).

Practical principles for Christian living

What are some practical principles for Christian living? Christians must separate themselves from all things that are not true, honest, just, pure, lovely, and of good report. They will avoid:

- Dishonesty of every kind: lying, stealing, cheating, being unfair, intent to deceive, gossip, slander, and betrayal.

- Impurity of every kind: fornication, adultery, incest, perversion, pornography, off-color jokes, profanity laden music, movies, television shows, and media.

- Places where we would never invite Jesus to accompany us such as nightclubs, strip bars, saloons, casinos, etc.

Whatever things are true, whatever things are noble, whatever things are just, whatever things are pure, whatever things are lovely, whatever things are of good report, if there is any virtue and if there is anything praiseworthy – meditate on these things. (Philippians 4:8)

Before anyone reading this book might want to accuse me of being legalistic, please read on. As a matter of full disclosure, in my younger days, I was once an aspiring actor and a heavy metal musician in Hollywood and New York. After hitting rock bottom due to drug and alcohol abuse, I received Jesus Christ as my personal Savior and Lord in 1988. My life has never been the same, and there's no turning back! That being said, there are many types and genres of secular music that have been largely captured by Satan. Lyrics often glorify vice and destroy a desire for spiritual things... the things of God. We've heard of newly converted people from other nations who tell us in "modern" western society, that our secular music is pretty much the same kind they used in witchcraft and the worship of false gods. My friend, any music you are not sure about should be abandoned. When we truly fall in love with Jesus, He changes everything, including our musical desires:

He has put a new song in my mouth—praise to our God; many will see it and fear, and will trust in the Lord (Psalm 40:3)

God has provided for His children plenty of good music that inspires, refreshes, elevates, and strengthens the Christian experience.

We must also be aware that worldly, sexually suggestive dancing inevitably leads us away from Jesus and true spirituality. Think about it: when the Israelites danced around the golden calf, it was idol worship because they had forgotten God (Exodus 32:17-24). When the daughter of Herodias danced before a drunken King Herod, John the Baptist was beheaded (Matthew 14:6-10).

Do things you watch on TV, or in theaters, and especially on the internet appeal to your lower or higher nature? Do they lead you to a greater love for Jesus or for the world? Do they glorify Jesus or enflame Satanic vices? Even non-Christians speak out against many TV and film productions. Satan has captured the eyes and ears of billions and as a result, is rapidly turning the world into a cesspool of crime, immorality, and hopelessness. One study revealed that without TV, "there would be 10,000 fewer murders per year in the USA, 70,000 fewer rapes, and 700,000 fewer assaults."[1] Jesus Christ, who loves you, asks you to take your eyes off Satan's thought-controllers and fix your eyes on Him.

Look to Me, and be saved, all you, ends of the earth! (Isaiah 45:22)

Actually, a safe guideline for viewing anything is to ask, "Would I feel comfortable inviting Jesus to watch the program with me?"

The works of the flesh are evident, which are: adultery, fornication, uncleanness, lewdness, idolatry, sorcery, hatred, contentions, jealousies, outbursts of wrath, selfish ambitions, dissensions, heresies, envy, murders, drunkenness, revelries, and the like; of which I tell you beforehand, just as I also told you in time past, that those who practice such things will not inherit the kingdom of God. (Galatians 5:19-21)

The infallible, inerrant Word of God is too clear to misunderstand. If a family should ban all TV programs that exhibit or condone any of the above sins, there would be very little to watch. If Jesus came to visit you, which TV shows or movies would you feel comfortable asking Him to view with you? All other shows are probably wrong for Christian viewing.

Many today feel capable of making spiritual decisions without input from anyone, including Jesus. What does Jesus say about such people? Listen to the Bible's unequivocal statements:

You shall not at all do as we are doing here today—every man doing whatever is right in his own eyes. (Deuteronomy 12:8)

There is a way that seems right to a man, but its end is the way of death. (Proverbs 16:25)

The way of a fool is right in his own eyes, but he who heeds counsel is wise. (Proverbs 12:15)

He who trusts in his own heart is a fool, but whoever walks wisely will be delivered. (Proverbs 28:26).

My choice of TV programs and my conduct must be guided by the exclusively by the words of Scripture—and not my own feelings.

Jesus gives solemn warnings regarding the example and influence of our lives upon others. There was a time when we all expected leaders, athletes, people of influence, and celebrities to set a good example, and use their influence wisely. However, in today's world, we are often disillusioned by the repugnant, irresponsible actions of those prominent individuals. Likewise, Jesus solemnly warns that Christians who disregard their own influence and example are in danger of leading people away from His kingdom.

Whoever causes one of these little ones who believe in Me to sin, it would be better for him if a millstone were hung around his neck, and he drowned in the depth of the sea (Matthew 18:6).

Therefore, let us not judge one another anymore, but rather resolve this, not to put a stumbling block or a cause to fall in our brother's way. (Romans 14:13)

None of us lives to himself. (Romans 14:7)

How does conduct and obedience relate to one's eternal salvation? The first epistle of John talks about Christian conduct. At its close (1 John 5:21), Jesus warns us through

His servant, John to keep ourselves from idols. The Master here is referring to anything that interferes with, or lessens our love for Him—such as fashion, possessions, adornment, evil forms of entertainment, etc. The natural fruit, or result, of a true conversion is to follow Jesus happily and adopt His lifestyle.

Should we expect everyone to look with approval upon the Christian lifestyle? The answer is no. In fact, we are and will continue to be hated by the world. Jesus said that the things of God are foolishness to the world because people lack spiritual discernment (1 Corinthians 2:14). When Jesus refers to conduct, He is laying down principles for those who are seeking to be led by His Spirit. His people will be grateful and will joyously follow His counsel. Many will not understand or approve.

How would a person who rejects Jesus' standards for conduct view heaven? Think about it: Such people would be miserable in heaven. There would be no nightclubs, booze, pornography, profanity, or gambling. Heaven would be "hell" for those who have not formed a true love relationship with Jesus. Christian standards make no sense to them (2 Corinthians 6:14-17).

Another question that many of God's people ask in our day is this, "How can I follow these Bible guidelines without appearing judgmental or legalistic?" All that we do should be with one motivation: to express love for Jesus and walk in His love (1 John 3:22). When Jesus is exalted and revealed to people through our lives (John 12:32), many will be drawn to Him. Our one question should always be, "Will this [music, drink, TV show, movie, book, etc.] honor Jesus?" We must sense Jesus' presence in every facet and activity of our lives. When we spend time with Him, we become like Him (2 Corinthians 3:18) – and the people around will respond to us as they did to the disciples of old:

They marveled and they realized that they had been with Jesus. (Acts 4:13)

Christians who live like that will never become pharisaical, judgmental, or legalistic. In Old Testament times, God's people were in almost constant apostasy because they chose to live as their heathen neighbors rather than follow the distinctive lifestyle God outlined for them (Deuteronomy 31:16; Judges 2:16; 1 Chronicles 5:25; Ezekiel 23:30). It is true today as well. No one can serve two masters (Matthew 6:24). Those who cling to the world and its mores will be slowly molded by Satan to adopt his desires and thus be programmed to reject heaven and be lost. In contrast, those who follow Jesus' principles for conduct will be changed into His image and prepared for heaven. There is no middle ground: We are either with Him or against Him.

Do you want to love Christ so much that to follow His principles for Christian living will be a joy and delight? Let's make a quality decision to live and walk by faith in Him, because the Bible says that "without faith, it is impossible to please God."

Reference

[1] "Violence, Reel to Reel." *Newsweek.* December 11, 1995

Anthony Sluzas

10
I Have Decided to Follow Jesus...
No Turning Back

HAVE you ever gone skydiving, or just prefer to watch? In either case, we know that when a skydiver steps to the edge of the aircraft door and leaps away from the plane, he knows, "Hey, there's no turning back!" He's gone too far, and if he should forget to strap on a parachute, nothing can save him and he will certainly plummet to a terrifying death. That would be a tragedy. But there is something even worse that can happen to a person. Indeed, it is far worse to come to the point of no return in your relationship with God. Yet millions are approaching this point and have no idea just how far they've fallen. Is it possible that you are one of them? What is the awful sin that could lead to such a fate? Why can't God forgive it? For a clear and penetrating answer—that is also at the same time, full of hope—take just a few minutes to read on.

Conviction and sin

What is the sin that God cannot forgive? Jesus said:

Every sin and blasphemy will be forgiven men, but the blasphemy against the Spirit will not be forgiven men.

(Matthew 12:31)

The sin God cannot forgive is "blasphemy against the Holy Spirit." People have many differing beliefs about this sin. Some believe it is cursing the Holy Spirit, some think it is murder, abortion, or suicide, sexual crimes, the denial of Christ, or worshiping a false god. But what does the Bible say about sin and blasphemy? The Bible says that all kinds of sin and blasphemy will be forgiven. So, none of the sins listed above is the sin that God cannot forgive. No single act of any kind is the unpardonable sin. It may sound contradictory, but both of the following statements are true:

- Sin and blasphemy will be forgiven.

- The blasphemy or sin against the Holy Spirit will not be forgiven.

Jesus made both statements in Matthew 12:31, so there is no error here. In order to harmonize these statements, we must discover the work of the Holy Spirit. What is the work of the Holy Spirit?

He [the Holy Spirit] will convict the world of sin, and of righteousness, and of judgment... He will guide you into all truth. (John 16:8,13)

The work of the Holy Spirit is to convict us of sin and to guide us into all truth. The Holy Spirit is God's agency for conversion. Without the Holy Spirit, no one feels sorrow for sin, nor is anyone ever converted.

When the Holy Spirit convicts us of sin, what must we do to be forgiven? When convicted of sin by the Holy Spirit, we must confess and turn from our sins in order to be forgiven. When we confess them, God not only forgives, but He also cleanses us from all unrighteousness. God is waiting and ready to forgive you for any and every sin you could commit (Psalm 86:5), but only if you confess and forsake it.

If we confess our sins, He is faithful and just to forgive us our sins and to cleanse us from all unrighteousness. (1 John 1:9)

What happens if we do not confess our sins when convicted by the Holy Spirit? If we do not confess our sins, Jesus cannot forgive our sins. Thus, any sin that we do not confess in unpardonable until we confess it, because forgiveness always follows confession. It never precedes it.

He who covers his sins will not prosper, but whoever confesses and forsakes them will have mercy. (Proverbs 28:13).

Resisting the Holy Spirit is terribly dangerous because it can eventually degenerate into backsliding, and total rejection of the Holy Spirit, which is the sin God can never forgive. It is passing the point of no return. The Holy Spirit is the only agency given to bring us conviction of sin in our hearts, and repentance. If we permanently reject Him, our case is thereafter hopeless. This subject is so important that God illustrates and explains it many different ways in Scripture.

As the Holy Spirit convicts us of sin or leads us to new truth, when should we act? The Bible repeatedly states that when we are convicted of sin, we must confess it at once. And when we're illuminated with learn new truth from God, we must accept it without delay. God's Word says:

I made haste, and did not delay to keep Your commandments. (Psalm 119:60)

Behold, now is the accepted time; behold, now is the day of salvation. (2 Corinthians 6:2)

Why are you waiting? Arise and be baptized, and wash away your sins, calling on the name of the Lord. (Acts 22:16)

What solemn warning does God give about the pleading of His Holy Spirit?

My Spirit will not strive with man forever. (Genesis 6:3)

God warned the people in Noah's day that His Holy Spirit would not keep pleading with them forever; nor will He today. God solemnly warns us as well that the Holy Spirit does not indefinitely continue pleading with a person to turn from sin and obey God.

Therefore, I speak to them in parables, because... hearing, they do not hear. (Matthew 13:13)

Is there a point when the Holy Spirit stops pleading with a person? The Holy Spirit stops talking to a person when that individual becomes deaf to His voice. The Bible describes it as hearing, but not hearing. There is no point in setting an alarm clock in a deaf person's room. He won't hear it. Likewise, a person can condition himself to not hear an alarm clock ring by repeatedly shutting it off and not getting up. The day finally comes when the alarm clock goes off and he doesn't hear it anymore.

Dear friend, please don't shut off the Holy Spirit! If we keep shutting Him off, one day He will speak to us and we will not hear Him. When that day comes, the Spirit sadly turns away from us because we have become deaf to His pleadings. We eventually pass the point of no return.

<u>Can any sin become the sin against the Holy Spirit?</u>

If we steadfastly refuse to confess and forsake any sin, we will eventually become deaf to the Holy Spirit's pleading and thus pass the point of no return. When the Spirit makes His appeal, we can choose to respond or reject it, but we cannot choose the consequences. They are fixed. If we consistently respond obediently, we will become like Jesus. The Holy Spirit will seal, or mark, us in the forehead as a child of God (Revelation 7:2-3), and thus assure us a place in God's heavenly kingdom. However, if we persistently refuse to respond, we will grieve away the Holy Spirit—and He will leave us forever, sealing our doom.

After King David committed the terrible double sin of adultery and murder, what anguished prayer did he pray? He pleaded with God not to take the Holy Spirit from him. Why was that? Because David knew if the Holy Spirit left him, he was doomed from that moment. He knew that only the Holy Spirit could lead him to repentance and restoration, and he trembled at the thought of becoming deaf to His voice. The Bible tells us in another place that God finally left Ephraim alone because he was joined to his idols (Hosea 4:17) and would not listen to the Spirit. He had become spiritually deaf. The most tragic thing that can happen to a person is for God to turn and leave him alone that man or woman's own devices. Don't let it happen to you!

What serious command did the apostle Paul give to the church in Thessalonica? He said:

Do not quench the Spirit. (1 Thessalonians 5:19).

The Spirit's pleading is like a holy fire burning in a person's mind and heart. Sin has the same effect on the Holy Spirit as water has upon fire. As we ignore the Holy Spirit and continue in sin, we pour water on the fire of the Holy Spirit. Paul's weighty words to the Thessalonians also apply to us today. Don't quench the fire of the Holy Spirit by repeatedly refusing to obey the Spirit's voice. If the fire goes out, we have passed the point of no return. Any unconfessed or unforsaken sin can ultimately snuff out the fire of the Holy Spirit. It could be the abuse of alcohol and/or drugs. It could be any form of immorality. It could be the absolute refusal to forgive one who has betrayed or otherwise injured you. Refusal to obey the Holy Spirit's voice in any area pours water on the fire of the Spirit. Don't put out the fire. No greater tragedy could take place.

What other powerful statement did Paul make to the Thessalonian believers?

With all unrighteous deception among those who perish, because they did not receive the love of the truth, that they might be saved. And for this reason, God will send them strong delusion, that they should believe the lie, that they all may be condemned who did not believe the truth but had pleasure in unrighteousness. (2 Thessalonians 2:10-12)

These are powerful and sobering words. God says that those who refuse to receive the truth and conviction brought by the Holy Spirit will—after the Spirit departs from them—receive a strong delusion to believe that error is truth. That's sobering thought, because we see it happening today.

What experience will those who have been sent these strong delusions face before the throne of God in the judgment?

Many will say to Me in that day, 'Lord, Lord, have we not prophesied in Your name, cast out demons in Your name, and done many wonders in Your name?' And then I will declare to them, 'I never knew you; depart from Me, you who practice lawlessness!' (Matthew 7:22-23).

Those who are crying out, "Lord, Lord" will be shocked that they are shut out. They'll be vehemently claiming that they were saved, and that they did this and that for the Lord. Jesus will then doubtless remind them of that crucial time in their lives when the Holy Spirit brought new truth and conviction. It was crystal clear it was the truth. It kept them awake at night as they wrestled over a decision. How their hearts burned within them! Finally, they said, "No!" They refused to listen any further to the Holy Spirit. Then came a strong delusion that caused them to feel saved when they were lost. Is there any greater tragedy?

Not everyone who says to Me, 'Lord, Lord,' shall enter the kingdom of heaven, but he who does the will of My Father in heaven. (Matthew 7:21)

All of us desire the blessed assurance of salvation, and God does want to save us! However, there is also a false sense of security sweeping much of the church that promises salvation while they continue living in sin and manifest no change whatsoever in their lives. Jesus said that true assurance is for those who do His Father's will. When we genuinely accept Jesus as Savior and Lord of our lives, then our lifestyles will change. We will become a totally new creation (2 Corinthians 5:17). We will gladly keep His commandments (John 14:15), and obediently follow where He leads (1 Peter 2:21). His resurrection power (Philippians 3:10) transforms us into His image (2 Corinthians 3:18). His wonderful peace floods our lives (John 14:27). With Jesus dwelling in us by His Spirit (Ephesians 3:16-17), we can do all things (Philippians 4:13) and "nothing will be impossible" (Matthew 17:20). Trust and obey!

A true assurance

As we follow where our Savior leads, He promises that no one can take us out of His hand (John 10:28) and that a crown of life awaits us (Revelation 2:10). What a glorious and genuine security Jesus gives His followers to experience! Assurance promised under any other conditions outside of Jesus Christ and the Cross is counterfeit, and will lead people to be lost for eternity (Proverbs 16:25).

Here is God's blessed promise to His faithful children who make Him Lord of their lives:

He Who has begun a good work in you will complete it until the day of Jesus Christ... for it is God Who works in you both to will and to do for His good pleasure. (Philippians 1:6; 2:13).

All of those who make Jesus their personal Savior and Lord are promised the miracles of the Lord that will see them safely through to His eternal kingdom forever. You just can't beat that!

Behold, I stand at the door and knock. If anyone hears My voice and opens the door, I will come in to him and dine with him, and he with Me. (Revelation 3:20)

Our Blessed Savior promises to enter our lives when we open our hearts to receive Him. It is Christ Who knocks on the door of your heart through His Holy Spirit. He comes and dwells in you for sweet fellowship, loving visits, and loving guidance and counsel. Heaven forbid we should ever be too busy or disinterested to form a warm, loving, and lasting friendship with our Lord. Jesus' close friends will be in no danger of being rejected on the day of judgment, and Christ will personally welcome them into His kingdom (Matthew 25:34)!

Will you decide now to always open the door of your heart as Jesus knocks, and will you be willing to follow where He leads? The decision is yours.

God loves you – no matter who you are, and no matter what you've done in the past. God loves you so much that gave His only begotten Son for you. The Bible tells us that:

...whoever believes in Him shall not perish but have everlasting life. (John 3:16)

Jesus laid down His life and rose again so that we could spend eternity with Him in heaven and experience His absolute best on earth. Would you like to accept Jesus Christ into your heart and life? With all your heart, say the following prayer out loud and mean from your heart.

"Dear Heavenly Father, I come to You now, admitting that I am a sinner. Right now, I choose to turn away from all my sin, and I ask You to cleanse me from all unrighteousness. I believe that Your Son, Jesus Christ, died on the cross to take away my sins. I also believe that He rose again from the dead so that I might be completely forgiven and made righteous through faith in Him. I call upon the name of Jesus Christ to be the Savior and Lord of my life. Jesus, I choose to follow You, and ask that You fill me with the power of the Holy Spirit. I declare that right now, I am a child of God. I am free from sin and full of the righteousness of God. I am saved in Jesus' Name. Amen.

If you have prayed this prayer to receive Jesus Christ as your Savior and Lord for the first time, please contact us on the web at:

YOURPLACEOFGRACE.COM

About the Author

Rev. Anthony Sluzas is a traveling evangelist and revivalist. He is the founder of Your Place Of Grace Ministries. His testimony is one of deliverance from emotional and physical abuse which he experienced as a child in parochial school, and substance abuse as a young aspiring actor/musician in Hollywood. While there, Anthony played several tiny bits on the sitcoms, *Three's Company*, *The Two of Us*, and appeared in numerous live theatrical productions.

He crashed and burned emotionally and spiritually in 1987, but the following year experienced a radical transformation in his heart and life when he accepted Jesus as his Lord and Savior while listening to E.V. Hill on TBN. God has worked miracles in Anthony's life and He can do the same for anyone and everyone through Jesus Christ.

Anthony served as Lead Pastor in several Assemblies of God churches from 1994-2010. Since 2010, Anthony has ministered from America's east coast to west coast and points in between. Anthony preaches and teaches the Message of Grace and Faith through the cross of Christ. He is called to win souls for Christ, and he focuses on God's Word in the areas of forgiveness, healing, and deliverance. Anthony loves to serve pastors, no matter the denomination, through prayer and a hand of friendship because he too was a pastor for years. Now, for over a decade, Anthony Sluzas has worked as a traveling evangelist and revivalist. His heart's desire is to minister to and point the way for those whom the world considers "lost causes" just like he was, to the Lord Jesus Christ.

For more information about Your Place of Grace Ministries, visit Anthony Sluzas's website at:

YOURPLACEOFGRACE.COM.

Also, be sure to download the "Your Place of Grace" app, available in both the Apple and Google play stores online.

Made in the USA
Columbia, SC
18 June 2020